TABLE OF CONTENTS

Mr. Rafael Martorell
11732 SW 9th Ct.
Pembroke Pnes, FL 33025

Secret Key #1 – Time is Your Greatest Enemy

Success Strategy #1

Pace Yourself

Wear a watch to the PHR Test. At the beginning of the test, check the time (or start a chronometer on your watch to count the minutes), and check the time after each passage or every few questions to make sure you are "on schedule." For the computerized test an onscreen clock display will keep track of your remaining time, but it may be easier for you to monitor your pace based on how many minutes have been used, rather than how many minutes remain.

If you are forced to speed up, do it efficiently. Usually one or more answer choices can be eliminated without too much difficulty. Above all, don't panic. Don't speed up and just begin guessing at random choices. By pacing yourself, and continually monitoring your progress against the clock or your watch, you will always know exactly how far ahead or behind you are with your available time. If you find that you are one minute behind on the test, don't skip one question without spending any time on it, just to catch back up. Spend perhaps 45 seconds on the question and after four questions, you will have caught back up more gradually. Once you catch back up, you can continue working each problem at your normal pace.

Furthermore, don't dwell on the problems that you were rushed on. If a problem was taking up too much time and you made a hurried guess, it must be difficult. The difficult questions are the ones you are most likely to miss anyway, so it isn't a big loss. It is better to end with more time than you need than to run out of time. You can always go back and work the problems that you skipped. If you have time left over, as you review the skipped questions, start at the earliest skipped question, spend at most another minute, and then move on to the next skipped question.

Lastly, sometimes it is beneficial to slow down if you are constantly getting ahead of time. You are always more likely to catch a careless mistake by working more slowly than quickly, and among very high-scoring test takers (those who are likely to have lots of time left over), careless errors affect the score more than mastery of material.

Secret Key #2 – Guessing is not Guesswork

You probably know that guessing is a good idea on the PHR test- unlike other standardized tests, there is no penalty for getting a wrong answer. Even if you have no idea about a question, you still have a 20-25% chance of getting it right.

Most test takers do not understand the impact that proper guessing can have on their score. Unless you score extremely high, guessing will significantly contribute to your final score.

Monkeys Take the PHR

What most test takers don't realize is that to insure that 20-25% chance, you have to guess randomly. If you put 20 monkeys in a room to take this test, assuming they answered once per question and behaved themselves, on average they would get 20-25% of the questions correct. Put 20 test takers in the room, and the average will be much lower among guessed questions. Why?

1. This test intentionally writes deceptive answer choices that "look" right. A test taker has no idea about a question, so picks the "best looking" answer, which is often wrong. The monkey has no idea what looks good and what doesn't, so will consistently be lucky about 20-25% of the time.
2. Test takers will eliminate answer choices from the guessing pool based on a hunch or intuition. Simple but correct answers often get excluded, leaving a 0% chance of being correct. The monkey has no clue, and often gets lucky with the best choice.

This is why the process of elimination endorsed by most test courses is flawed and detrimental to your performance- test takers don't guess, they make an ignorant stab in the dark that is usually worse than random.

Success Strategy #2

Let me introduce one of the most valuable ideas of this course- the $5 challenge:

You only mark your "best guess" if you are willing to bet $5 on it.
You only eliminate choices from guessing if you are willing to bet $5 on it.

Why $5? Five dollars is an amount of money that is small yet not insignificant, and can really add up fast (20 questions could cost you $100). Likewise, each answer choice on one question of the PHR will have a small impact on your overall score, but it can really add up to a lot of points in the end.

The process of elimination IS valuable. The following shows your chance of guessing it right:

If you eliminate this many choices:	0	1	2	3	4
Chance of getting it correct	20%	25%	33%	50%	100%

However, if you accidentally eliminate the right answer or go on a hunch for an incorrect answer, your chances drop dramatically: to 0%. By guessing among all the answer choices, you are GUARANTEED to have a shot at the right answer.

That's why the $5 test is so valuable- if you give up the advantage and safety of a pure guess, it had better be worth the risk.

What we still haven't covered is how to be sure that whatever guess you make is truly random. Here's the easiest way:

Always pick the first answer choice among those remaining.

Such a technique means that you have decided, **before you see a single test question**, exactly how you are going to guess- and since the order of choices tells you nothing about which one is correct, this guessing technique is perfectly random.

Secret Key #3 – Practice Smarter, Not Harder

Many test takers delay the test preparation process because they dread the awful amounts of practice time they think necessary to succeed on the test. We have refined an effective method that will take you only a fraction of the time.

There are a number of "obstacles" in your way on the PHR test. Among these are answering questions, finishing in time, and mastering test-taking strategies. All must be executed on the day of the test at peak performance, or your score will suffer. The PHR is a mental marathon that has a large impact on your future.

Just like a marathon runner, it is important to work your way up to the full challenge. So first you just worry about questions, and then time, and finally strategy:

Success Strategy

1. Find a good source for practice tests.
2. If you are willing to make a larger time investment, consider using more than one study guide- often the different approaches of multiple authors will help you "get" difficult concepts.
3. Take a practice test with no time constraints, with all study helps "open book." Take your time with questions and focus on applying strategies.
4. Take a practice test with time constraints, with all guides "open book."
5. Take a final practice test with no open material and time limits

If you have time to take more practice tests, just repeat step 5. By gradually exposing yourself to the full rigors of the test environment, you will condition your mind to the stress of test day and maximize your success.

Secret Key #4 - Prepare, Don't Procrastinate

Let me state an obvious fact: if you take the test three times, you will get three different scores. This is due to the way you feel on test day, the level of preparedness you have, and, despite the test writers' claims to the contrary, some tests WILL be easier for you than others.

Since your future depends so much on your score, you should maximize your chances of success. In order to maximize the likelihood of success, you've got to prepare in advance. This means taking practice tests and spending time learning the information and test taking strategies you will need to succeed.

Never take the test as a "practice" test, expecting that you can just take it again if you need to. Feel free to take sample tests on your own, but when you go to take the official test, be prepared, be focused, and do your best the first time!

Secret Key #5 - Test Yourself

Everyone knows that time is money. There is no need to spend too much of your time or too little of your time preparing for the test. You should only spend as much of your precious time preparing as is necessary for you to get the score you need.

Once you have taken a practice test under real conditions of time constraints, then you will know if you are ready for the test or not.

If you have scored extremely high the first time that you take the practice test, then there is not much point in spending countless hours studying. You are already there.

Benchmark your abilities by retaking practice tests and seeing how much you have improved. Once you score high enough to guarantee success, then you are ready.

If you have scored well below where you need, then knuckle down and begin studying in earnest. Check your improvement regularly through the use of practice tests under real conditions. Above all, don't worry, panic, or give up. The key is perseverance!

Then, when you go to take the test, remain confident and remember how well you did on the practice tests. If you can score high enough on a practice test, then you can do the same on the real thing.

Top 20 Test Taking Tips

1. Carefully follow all the test registration procedures
2. Know the test directions, duration, topics, question types, how many questions
3. Setup a flexible study schedule at least 3-4 weeks before test day
4. Study during the time of day you are most alert, relaxed, and stress free
5. Maximize your learning style; visual learner use visual study aids, auditory learner use auditory study aids
6. Focus on your weakest knowledge base
7. Find a study partner to review with and help clarify questions
8. Practice, practice, practice
9. Get a good night's sleep; don't try to cram the night before the test
10. Eat a well balanced meal
11. Know the exact physical location of the testing site; drive the route to the site prior to test day
12. Bring a set of ear plugs; the testing center could be noisy
13. Wear comfortable, loose fitting, layered clothing to the testing center; prepare for it to be either cold or hot during the test
14. Bring at least 2 current forms of ID to the testing center
15. Arrive to the test early; be prepared to wait and be patient
16. Eliminate the obviously wrong answer choices, then guess the first remaining choice
17. Pace yourself; don't rush, but keep working and move on if you get stuck
18. Maintain a positive attitude even if the test is going poorly
19. Keep your first answer unless you are positive it is wrong
20. Check your work, don't make a careless mistake

General Strategies

The most important thing you can do is to ignore your fears and jump into the test immediately- do not be overwhelmed by any strange-sounding terms. You have to jump into the test like jumping into a pool- all at once is the easiest way.

Make Predictions

As you read and understand the question, try to guess what the answer will be. Remember that several of the answer choices are wrong, and once you begin reading them, your mind will immediately become cluttered with answer choices designed to throw you off. Your mind is typically the most focused immediately after you have read the question and digested its contents. If you can, try to predict what the correct answer will be. You may be surprised at what you can predict.

Quickly scan the choices and see if your prediction is in the listed answer choices. If it is, then you can be quite confident that you have the right answer. It still won't hurt to check the other answer choices, but most of the time, you've got it!

Answer the Question

It may seem obvious to only pick answer choices that answer the question, but the test writers can create some excellent answer choices that are wrong. Don't pick an answer just because it sounds right, or you believe it to be true. It MUST answer the question. Once you've made your selection, always go back and check it against the question and make sure that you didn't misread the question, and the answer choice does answer the question posed.

Benchmark

After you read the first answer choice, decide if you think it sounds correct or not. If it doesn't, move on to the next answer choice. If it does, mentally mark that answer choice. This doesn't mean that you've definitely selected it as your answer choice, it just means that it's the best you've seen thus far. Go ahead and read the next choice. If the next choice is worse than the one you've already selected, keep going to the next answer choice. If the next choice is better than the choice you've already selected, mentally mark the new answer choice as your best guess.

The first answer choice that you select becomes your standard. Every other answer choice must be benchmarked against that standard. That choice is correct until proven otherwise by another answer choice beating it out. Once you've decided that no other answer choice seems as good, do one final check to ensure that your answer choice answers the question posed.

Valid Information

Don't discount any of the information provided in the question. Every piece of information may be necessary to determine the correct answer. None of the information in the question is there to throw you off (while the answer choices will certainly have information to throw you off). If two

Copyright © Mometrix Media. You have been licensed one copy of this document for personal use only. Any other reproduction or redistribution is strictly prohibited. All rights reserved.

seemingly unrelated topics are discussed, don't ignore either. You can be confident there is a relationship, or it wouldn't be included in the question, and you are probably going to have to determine what is that relationship to find the answer.

Avoid "Fact Traps"

Don't get distracted by a choice that is factually true. Your search is for the answer that answers the question. Stay focused and don't fall for an answer that is true but incorrect. Always go back to the question and make sure you're choosing an answer that actually answers the question and is not just a true statement. An answer can be factually correct, but it MUST answer the question asked. Additionally, two answers can both be seemingly correct, so be sure to read all of the answer choices, and make sure that you get the one that BEST answers the question.

Milk the Question

Some of the questions may throw you completely off. They might deal with a subject you have not been exposed to, or one that you haven't reviewed in years. While your lack of knowledge about the subject will be a hindrance, the question itself can give you many clues that will help you find the correct answer. Read the question carefully and look for clues. Watch particularly for adjectives and nouns describing difficult terms or words that you don't recognize. Regardless of if you completely understand a word or not, replacing it with a synonym either provided or one you more familiar with may help you to understand what the questions are asking. Rather than wracking your mind about specific detailed information concerning a difficult term or word, try to use mental substitutes that are easier to understand.

The Trap of Familiarity

Don't just choose a word because you recognize it. On difficult questions, you may not recognize a number of words in the answer choices. The test writers don't put "make-believe" words on the test; so don't think that just because you only recognize all the words in one answer choice means that answer choice must be correct. If you only recognize words in one answer choice, then focus on that one. Is it correct? Try your best to determine if it is correct. If it is, that is great, but if it doesn't, eliminate it. Each word and answer choice you eliminate increases your chances of getting the question correct, even if you then have to guess among the unfamiliar choices.

Eliminate Answers

Eliminate choices as soon as you realize they are wrong. But be careful! Make sure you consider all of the possible answer choices. Just because one appears right, doesn't mean that the next one won't be even better! The test writers will usually put more than one good answer choice for every question, so read all of them. Don't worry if you are stuck between two that seem right. By getting down to just two remaining possible choices, your odds are now 50/50. Rather than wasting too much time, play the odds. You are guessing, but guessing wisely, because you've been able to knock out some of the answer choices that you know are wrong. If you are eliminating choices and realize that the last answer choice you are left with is also obviously wrong, don't panic. Start over and consider each choice again. There may easily be something that you missed the first time and will realize on the second pass.

Tough Questions

If you are stumped on a problem or it appears too hard or too difficult, don't waste time. Move on! Remember though, if you can quickly check for obviously incorrect answer choices, your chances of guessing correctly are greatly improved. Before you completely give up, at least try to knock out a couple of possible answers. Eliminate what you can and then guess at the remaining answer choices before moving on.

Brainstorm

If you get stuck on a difficult question, spend a few seconds quickly brainstorming. Run through the complete list of possible answer choices. Look at each choice and ask yourself, "Could this answer the question satisfactorily?" Go through each answer choice and consider it independently of the other. By systematically going through all possibilities, you may find something that you would otherwise overlook. Remember that when you get stuck, it's important to try to keep moving.

Read Carefully

Understand the problem. Read the question and answer choices carefully. Don't miss the question because you misread the terms. You have plenty of time to read each question thoroughly and make sure you understand what is being asked. Yet a happy medium must be attained, so don't waste too much time. You must read carefully, but efficiently.

Face Value

When in doubt, use common sense. Always accept the situation in the problem at face value. Don't read too much into it. These problems will not require you to make huge leaps of logic. The test writers aren't trying to throw you off with a cheap trick. If you have to go beyond creativity and make a leap of logic in order to have an answer choice answer the question, then you should look at the other answer choices. Don't overcomplicate the problem by creating theoretical relationships or explanations that will warp time or space. These are normal problems rooted in reality. It's just that the applicable relationship or explanation may not be readily apparent and you have to figure things out. Use your common sense to interpret anything that isn't clear.

Prefixes

If you're having trouble with a word in the question or answer choices, try dissecting it. Take advantage of every clue that the word might include. Prefixes and suffixes can be a huge help. Usually they allow you to determine a basic meaning. Pre- means before, post- means after, pro - is positive, de- is negative. From these prefixes and suffixes, you can get an idea of the general meaning of the word and try to put it into context. Beware though of any traps. Just because con is the opposite of pro, doesn't necessarily mean congress is the opposite of progress!

Hedge Phrases

Watch out for critical "hedge" phrases, such as likely, may, can, will often, sometimes, often, almost, mostly, usually, generally, rarely, sometimes. Question writers insert these hedge phrases to cover every possibility. Often an answer choice will be wrong simply because it leaves no room for exception. Avoid answer choices that have definitive words like "exactly," and "always".

- 13 -

Switchback Words

Stay alert for "switchbacks". These are the words and phrases frequently used to alert you to shifts in thought. The most common switchback word is "but". Others include although, however, nevertheless, on the other hand, even though, while, in spite of, despite, regardless of.

New Information

Correct answer choices will rarely have completely new information included. Answer choices typically are straightforward reflections of the material asked about and will directly relate to the question. If a new piece of information is included in an answer choice that doesn't even seem to relate to the topic being asked about, then that answer choice is likely incorrect. All of the information needed to answer the question is usually provided for you, and so you should not have to make guesses that are unsupported or choose answer choices that require unknown information that cannot be reasoned on its own.

Time Management

On technical questions, don't get lost on the technical terms. Don't spend too much time on any one question. If you don't know what a term means, then since you don't have a dictionary, odds are you aren't going to get much further. You should immediately recognize terms as whether or not you know them. If you don't, work with the other clues that you have, the other answer choices and terms provided, but don't waste too much time trying to figure out a difficult term.

Contextual Clues

Look for contextual clues. An answer can be right but not correct. The contextual clues will help you find the answer that is most right and is correct. Understand the context in which a phrase or statement is made. This will help you make important distinctions.

Don't Panic

Panicking will not answer any questions for you. Therefore, it isn't helpful. When you first see the question, if your mind goes blank, take a deep breath. Force yourself to mechanically go through the steps of solving the problem and using the strategies you've learned.

Pace Yourself

Don't get clock fever. It's easy to be overwhelmed when you're looking at a page full of questions, your mind is full of random thoughts and feeling confused, and the clock is ticking down faster than you would like. Calm down and maintain the pace that you have set for yourself. As long as you are on track by monitoring your pace, you are guaranteed to have enough time for yourself. When you get to the last few minutes of the test, it may seem like you won't have enough time left, but if you only have as many questions as you should have left at that point, then you're right on track!

Answer Selection

The best way to pick an answer choice is to eliminate all of those that are wrong, until only one is left and confirm that is the correct answer. Sometimes though, an answer choice may immediately look right. Be careful! Take a second to make sure that the other choices are not equally obvious. Don't make a hasty mistake. There are only two times that you should stop before checking other answers. First is when you are positive that the answer choice you have selected is correct. Second is when time is almost out and you have to make a quick guess!

Check Your Work

Since you will probably not know every term listed and the answer to every question, it is important that you get credit for the ones that you do know. Don't miss any questions through careless mistakes. If at all possible, try to take a second to look back over your answer selection and make sure you've selected the correct answer choice and haven't made a costly careless mistake (such as marking an answer choice that you didn't mean to mark). This quick double check should more than pay for itself in caught mistakes for the time it costs.

Beware of Directly Quoted Answers

Sometimes an answer choice will repeat word for word a portion of the question or reference section. However, beware of such exact duplication – it may be a trap! More than likely, the correct choice will paraphrase or summarize a point, rather than being exactly the same wording.

Slang

Scientific sounding answers are better than slang ones. An answer choice that begins "To compare the outcomes…" is much more likely to be correct than one that begins "Because some people insisted…"

Extreme Statements

Avoid wild answers that throw out highly controversial ideas that are proclaimed as established fact. An answer choice that states the "process should used in certain situations, if…" is much more likely to be correct than one that states the "process should be discontinued completely." The first is a calm rational statement and doesn't even make a definitive, uncompromising stance, using a hedge word "if" to provide wiggle room, whereas the second choice is a radical idea and far more extreme.

Answer Choice Families

When you have two or more answer choices that are direct opposites or parallels, one of them is usually the correct answer. For instance, if one answer choice states "x increases" and another answer choice states "x decreases" or "y increases," then those two or three answer choices are very similar in construction and fall into the same family of answer choices. A family of answer choices is when two or three answer choices are very similar in construction, and yet often have a directly opposite meaning. Usually the correct answer choice will be in that family of answer choices. The "odd man out" or answer choice that doesn't seem to fit the parallel construction of the other answer choices is more likely to be incorrect.

Why Certify?

PHR: **Professional in Human Resources**
SPHR: **Senior Professional in Human Resources**

- Raise the standards in your field and distinguish your experience.
- Use your credentials to further your career.
- Improve your skills and abilities to manage workers

Candidate Handbook
http://www.hrci.org/AboutUs/HB/

Score

The passing score for each exam (based on a scaled score) is 500. The minimum possible score is 100. The maximum possible score is 700.

Question Types

The PHR exams are multiple choice and consist of 200 scored questions plus 25 pretest questions randomly distributed throughout the exam (a total of 225 questions). Each question lists four possible answers, only one of which is the correct or "best possible answer." The answer to each question can be derived independently of the answer to any other question. Four hours are allotted to complete the exam.

Strategic Business Management

Mission and vision statements

Mission statements and vision statements are similar in that they are both intended to clarify the objectives of the organization. However, a mission statement is only intended to define the broad mission an organization is attempting to carry out on a daily basis. A vision statement is intended to define the specific goals an organization hopes to achieve in the future.

A mission statement is a declaration of the reason an organization exists. This is important in determining standards, values, strategies, and other organizational aspects and serves as a guideline for establishing the processes to achieve goals. For example, the mission statement of a retail chain might be "to provide the best shopping experience possible for our customers." As a result, a decision might be made to implement standards and practices that promote high levels of customer service.

A vision statement is a declaration of the goals the organization wishes to achieve at some future point, which is important in designing and implementing the strategies necessary to meet those goals. For example, the vision statement of a retail chain might be to become the largest retail chain in the United States. As a result, the decision might be made to implement strategies that allow for rapid expansion, like finding and purchasing new locations and training new personnel quickly.

Goals

There are a variety of ways to ensure specific goals are well-defined, valid, and useful. The most effective way is to use the acronym SMART: *specific, measurable, achievable, relevant, and time-related*. Valid goals should be specific and well-defined, able to be accurately measured, possible considering resources and environment, and relevant to overall objectives. A valid goal should also have a specific deadline to ensure it is completed efficiently and can be compared accurately with other goals.

Accounting and financial business metrics

Although there is a wide range of business metrics that measure performance, three of the most common accounting and financial business metrics are cash flow, return on investment (ROI), and return on equity (ROE.) Cash flow refers to the amount of money taken in compared to the amount of money spent during a given period. Return on investment is the amount of money earned from an investment compared to how much money was spent to make that investment, or the ratio between profit and loss. Return on equity is the amount of money made compared to the average investment of each shareholder.

There are a variety of ways to apply cash flow to strategic planning; however there are advantages to using a cash flow metric. Cash flow offers the opportunity to analyze exactly how much money is coming in and going out, and makes it easy to determine if money is being gained or lost over a given period. It is especially important to take the strategic plan into consideration if the organization is losing money. In order to show a profit by the end of the fiscal year, it is important to understand how much money is spent on a weekly or monthly basis and plan around those expenses by finding ways to reduce them, eliminate them, or earn enough to offset each expense.

There are a variety of ways an organization can apply a metric, such as the return or estimated return on an investment to the organization's strategic planning. However, the return or estimated return on a particular investment is usually used if an organization is attempting to decide between two investments. Because there are limited financial resources available to devote to expenses and investments, money must be spent on endeavors with the greatest return. If the return on each investment can be estimated or accurately identified, it is easy to create a strategic plan that will earn the most money.

Return on equity (ROE) is usually the foundation of an organization's strategic plan. This is because the primary goal of any business is to offer its shareholders the largest possible return on their investment. A for-profit organization's ROE is an indication of overall performance. Another strategy is to compare ROI with the ROI of other companies. If there is a competitive return, strategic plans should not be drastically changed, but if the ROI is much lower than competitors, a new strategy is in order.

Marketing and sales metrics

Three of the most common sales and marketing business metrics are the number of customers/orders for the period, the average amount received for each order, and the gross profit margin. The *number of customers/orders* is an exact or estimated count of the number of people purchasing products from the company or the number of orders the company has received during a specific period of time. The *average amount received for each order* is the total amount in dollars received for a particular period divided by the number of orders. Finally, the *gross profit margin* is the total revenue for a certain period of time minus the cost of sales for that particular period divided by the total revenue for that period.

The number of customers/orders received is usually used to identify problems with current marketing and sales strategies. If the number of customers or orders for a specific period is significantly lower than previous periods or the number of customers or orders is significantly lower than the numbers estimated from competitors, there may be a problem with the selling strategy. For example, owners of a fast food restaurant may decide to change their menu by adding and marketing healthier options to expand their customer base. If there is a sudden drop in the number of customers, the strategy is not working.

The average amount received per order is usually used to determine the effectiveness of marketing and sales strategies from their current customer base. The average amount received per order helps identify how much each customer is contributing to the organization's cash flow. This helps determine if the focus should be on expanding the customer base or encouraging the current customer base to spend more through marketing initiatives such as special sales, discounts, reward programs for frequent shoppers, etc.

The gross profit margin is usually used to help determine whether or not a particular marketing or sales strategy currently in effect is actually profitable. For example, a fast food restaurant chain may have instituted a new "less than a dollar" menu and a marketing campaign focusing on this menu a year ago. Comparing the gross profit margin for the current year with the previous year is helpful in determining if the new campaign is increasing sales or if a new strategy is needed.

Operations and business development metrics

Three of the most common operations and business development metrics used to measure performance are the number of activities, the opportunity success rate, and the innovation rate. The number of activities is an exact or estimated count of how many tasks the organization is attempting to do at one time. The opportunity success rate is the number of opportunities taken advantage of divided by the total number of opportunities available. Finally, the innovation rate is the gross revenue from new ideas, products, and services divided by the total gross revenue.

The number of activities is usually used to determine whether or not the company is taking on a larger workload than what the company can normally handle. Multitasking is an important part of any enterprise, but it is important to identify how much work is too much. For example, if an old-fashioned toy manufacturer priding itself on the fact that each toy is hand-crafted wants to start building a large array of modern toys, he may find that it is not possible to expand the without drastically increasing costs or eliminating other activities. This is because each old-fashioned toy takes a significant amount of time to construct and the company may not be able to expand its modern toy building activities without eliminating some of the old-fashioned toys from its product line.

An organization's opportunity success rate is useful for developing a strategic plan because it helps determine if available opportunities are being used effectively. If the opportunity success rate is low, the focus should be on strategies that boost sales. If the opportunity success rate is high, the focus should be on marketing strategies that expand customer base. However, even though an opportunity success rate is an indication of how the company itself is developing, it is closely linked to sales and marketing. As a result, it may not be wise for companies that have short pre-sale periods to use opportunity success rates because these rates can change greatly before new strategies are even implemented.

Innovation rate is useful for developing a strategic plan because it helps determine if new ideas, products, and services are profitable. If the innovation rate is *equal to or higher than* competitors, the current innovation strategy is appropriate and the focus should be on designing products and services similar to those recently placed on the market. On the other hand, if the innovation rate is significantly *lower* than competitors, a new innovation strategy should be implemented focusing on developing products and services not similar to those recently placed on the market. The innovation rate is not a measure of how innovative a company is, but rather a measure of how profitable each group of new innovations has actually been.

Information technology metrics

Three of the most common information technology metrics an organization might use are the number of online orders, the availability of information resources, and the number of views per page/listing. The number of online orders is a count of how many orders have been placed by customers using the company's website. The availability of information resources is the percentage of time the company's servers, websites, e-mail, and other technological resources are accessible at the time those resources are needed. The number of views per page/listing is a count of how many times customers have looked at a particular web page or online product.

The number of online orders placed using an organization's website can be useful for developing a strategic plan because it measures the effectiveness of their website. If the number of orders made online through their website or by e-mail is equal to or greater than the number of orders placed through traditional means (such as in a store or by phone), focus should be on maintaining or expanding online services. On the other hand, if the number of orders placed online is significantly less than the number of orders placed through more traditional means, strategies should be implemented to improve online services. It is also useful to compare the number of online orders made through their website to the number of online orders made through websites belonging to competitors to determine the effectiveness of the website in relation to the rest of the industry.

The availability of the organization's information resources is an essential factor to consider for any organization's strategic plan because technology is only useful if it is working. If the computer systems, websites, e-mail services, or other pieces of technology used by employees or customers normally are inaccessible, the organization will not be able to function normally. Identifying problems with IT systems and IT personnel minimizes future problems.

The number of views per page or views per listing for an organization's websites, ads, or other information resources is an important factor for an organization to consider during the strategic planning process because they measure the effectiveness of its websites and ads. If a listing receives a large number of views and a large number of customers place orders, those sites are performing well. However, if a listing is not receiving a large number of views or receiving a large number of views, but only a small percentage of the customers are buying the product, website marketing and design should be rethought.

General business and economic environment metrics

Three of the most common metrics related to the general business and economic environments an organization might use are the current number of competitors and the average number of new competitors entering the market per year, the organization's current market share, and the average income of customers in the target market. The current number of competitors is the number of other businesses within the same market. The average number of new competitors is the average number of businesses entering the same market during a year. The current market share is the percentage of the local or overall market the business controls, or the percentage of the market with which the organization usually does business. The average income of customers in the target market is the amount an average customer would normally make in a given year.

The current number of competitors in the market and the average number of new competitors entering the market per year is a useful set of statistics for organization's attempting to develop a strategic plan. The current number of competitors in the market measures how much competition is present in a particular market. The average number of new competitors entering the market per year is a good way to measure how that competition will change. In other words, these statistics help determine how much competition is in the market now and how much there will be in the near future. These statistics help in planning for the amount of competition likely to be faced and serve as a warning for potential problems in the market.

The organization's current market share is an important factor to consider during the strategic planning process because it measures success and growth in a particular market and compares that success and growth with competitors. As a result, the current market share is ultimately an indication of how the organization as a whole is performing in the current business environment for each specific market the organization is doing business. If an organization's market share is continuing to grow or is maintaining a large, stable market share, it is usually an indication current strategies are working. However, if market share is beginning to decline or is stable, but low when compared to competitors, then something new probably needs to be tried.

The average income of customers in the target market can be an important piece of information to consider during the strategic planning process because it analyzes the current economic environment. Because the amount of money individuals within the target market earn can fluctuate greatly, it is essential to ensure customers can afford to purchase the product. For example, if a car dealer is attempting to sell a line of new cars normally costing $25,000, it may be difficult to convince someone that just had their pay cut from $50,000 to $25,000 a year to purchase the car.

Sources of information

The three most common sources an organization might use to find information about common industry practices, industry developments, and technological developments are newspapers, magazines, and websites. Large newspapers that focus primarily on business will often publish articles that detail major changes occurring in each industry as well as articles detailing future technologies. Business magazines published by the particular industry the organization is a part of detail current trends. Industry websites detail changing trends and developments. Shareholder websites for competitors will often identify the practices and acquisitions on which competitors are focusing.

There are a variety of sources that an organization might use to find information about the current labor pool including newspapers, magazines, industry websites, and other similar print and online publications. Most major publications will print articles about major changes in the work force as soon as they occur. One of the most useful publications is the Occupational Outlook Handbook. The Occupational Outlook Handbook (OOH), which is published by the United States Bureau of Labor Statistics, is primarily designed for individuals seeking employment. However, it also provides detailed descriptions of each occupation, information about the current labor pool, and projections for the next five to ten years of how the labor pool for each occupation is expected to change.

There are a variety of sources an organization might use to find information about upcoming legislation and new regulations that might affect the particular industry that the organization is a part of, but the three most common sources are newspapers, magazines, and websites. Virtually every newspaper covers information related to upcoming legislation and large national newspapers can often be a good way to find out about changes to federal and state laws while smaller city newspapers can be a good way for an organization to find out about changes to laws and ordinances passed by the local government that may impact the organization. Industry magazines and publications are a useful tool for finding information about upcoming legislation of concern to members of the industry. Industry websites, government websites, and certain professional websites will usually detail the progress of legislation.

Legislative process

How bills become laws
The process of forming a new law begins with the bill being introduced by the Senate or the House of Representatives. The bill is then referred to a committee that determines if the bill should be considered further by a subcommittee, considered further by the entire floor of the House or Senate, or if the bill should be ignored. If the bill reaches the floor of the House or Senate, the bill is debated and a vote is taken to pass or defeat the bill. If the bill is passed in the Senate, then the bill is passed on to the House to be considered in the same way and vice versa. After both the House and Senate have approved a bill, the bill is sent to the president to be signed into law, vetoed, or returned to Congress. It may become law automatically if it is ignored for 10 days while Congress is in session, or die automatically if it is ignored until after Congress is in session.

Influencing legislation
There is a wide range of methods that an individual, such as an HR professional, might use to influence upcoming legislation, but the three most common methods are by mail, by scheduling meetings with elected officials, or by lobbying. To influence legislation by mail, a formal letter can be sent to an elected official such as a state senator, a congressman or congresswoman, a local mayor, etc. To influence legislation through meetings, a meeting should be scheduled with an elected official or a member of his or her staff to discuss the issue of concern. To influence legislation by lobbying, members of similar organizations, possibly even competitors within the same industry, should be found and the entire group should express their opinions to an appropriate elected official by mail or in person.

Functions of management

The five basic functions normally associated with management are planning, organizing, coordinating, directing, and controlling. Planning refers to the process of actually determining what the organization is attempting to achieve and how the organization is going to achieve that goal. Organizing refers to the process of obtaining and allocating human resources, financial resources, and similar resources to carry out the plan the organization has established. Coordinating refers to the process of making sure all allocated resources are functioning together as planned to achieve goals. Directing, sometimes referred to as leading, is the process of making sure the work associated with completing the goal is actually carried out in an effective manner. Finally, controlling is the process of evaluating the organization's progress towards the goal. It is the process where the manager actually has to determine if the plan is working.

Project management

Project management is the process of determining and implementing a plan that will lead to the completion of a particular task within defined constraints. It refers to the process of planning how to complete a project that meets quality standards, achieves predetermined tasks, and is completed within the time allowed and the financial limitations of the project. Project management makes it possible to prioritize the large number of projects most organizations attempt to accomplish.

The three main factors project managers traditionally have been expected to control while completing a project include the cost of the project, the time spent on the project, and the scope of the project. The cost of the project refers to the total amount of resources spent on the project including finances and raw materials. The time spent on the project refers to the total amount of time spent by the employees to complete that task. The scope of the project refers to the requirements needed to complete the task in an appropriate fashion. Project managers must make sure the project is completed within set time and cost constraints and the end result meets the organization's requirements.

An important factor a project manager might be expected to control on a regular basis is the risk associated with a project. Most projects carry some risk of failure and some risk of overspending and missing deadlines. It is essential for a project manager to find ways of minimizing these risks to avoid having a potentially significant negative impact on the organization.

It is also important for the project manager to monitor and control the quality of the work being performed to ensure the end result meets expectations, which is usually one of the main factors involved in controlling the scope of the project. Most tasks have specific requirements or guidelines that need to be met for the task to be completed correctly. If quality requirements are not met, the project manager has failed to meet the scope of the project.

Gantt chart

A Gantt chart is a type of bar chart often used to identify tasks involved in a project and to establish a schedule for completing those tasks. Gantt charts are closely related to Work Breakdown Structures because it breaks the larger project down into the specific activities and tasks. A Gantt chart lists each main task, referred to as a summary element, and then lists the subtasks that need to be completed to complete the main task, referred to as terminal elements, under the main task. Each task included on the chart has a bar next to it indicating how much of the task has been completed and a different colored bar indicating how much of the task is still remaining. Gantt charts also indicate the date or week each task started and when the project needs to be completed.

PERT

The Project Evaluation and Review Technique (PERT) is a method of determining how much time is required to complete a specific project. The PERT process consists of breaking the larger project into a series of separate tasks necessary to complete the larger project and then organizing each of these smaller tasks into a chart. Each task in the PERT chart is represented by a line or arrow drawn from a circle representing an event or goal (such as the project beginning or completing a task and moving onto the next task) to a circle representing the next event or goal. Each event or goal circle is assigned a number and the circles are arranged based on the order in which they are to be completed. The organization can then estimate the amount of time each task will take and note that estimate above the corresponding task line or arrow in the chart.

WBS

A Work Breakdown Structure (WBS) is a method for breaking a larger project down into a series of separate smaller tasks necessary to complete the larger project. The WBS is based on the100% Rule, which states that the subtasks included in a WBS must describe 100% of the work necessary to complete the larger task. Work Breakdown Structures are usually depicted in chart form as tree structures that start off with the larger task and then branch out to the subtasks that make up the larger task. Each subtask is then broken down further into smaller subtasks and each subtask is then assigned a percentage based on how much of the project is related specifically to that subtask.

Outsourcing

Outsourcing refers to the practice of hiring third-party companies or contractors to perform tasks traditionally performed by the organization itself. It is the process of finding people or organizations outside the organization to perform tasks that were originally done "in-house" by employees or other resources of the organization. There are a variety of situations it might be better to outsource, but some of the most important factors are the cost of performing the task in-house, the cost of a third-party performing the task, the level of difficulty associated with the task, the level of quality control necessary for the task, the level of quality control available from outside sources, the impact on the organization if the task is not completed when expected or as expected, and how much control the organization needs to maintain.

There are a variety of factors that an organization should consider before choosing a third-party vendor regardless of the specific task. However, four of the most important factors to consider are the costs associated with doing business with the vendor, the quality of the vendor's product or service, the ability of the vendor to meet the organization's needs for the specific task, and the vendor's experience as it relates to the specific task. The cost associated with a particular vendor refers to all of the costs potentially incurred with a particular vendor. The quality of the vendor's product or service refers to the vendor's ability to perform the service or manufacture the product to the standards set by the organization. Finally, the ability of the vendor to meet the organization's needs and the vendor's experience as it relates to the task are both ways of determining if the vendor will be able to consistently perform the task as expected.

Offshoring

Offshoring is a process similar to outsourcing because it refers to hiring an individual or company located in another country to perform a task the organization would normally perform domestically. It is the practice of hiring individuals or companies offshore, overseas, or in a different country to provide a product or service for the organization, usually because it can be more cost effective. Offshoring differs from outsourcing because it is possible to have an offshore division that is actually a part of the organization.

Insourcing

Insourcing is the opposite of outsourcing because it refers to the practice in which an organization performs a task "in-house" by hiring individuals as direct employees of the organization or by acquiring an outside company in order to perform a particular task that had been previously performed by outside vendors. In other words, insourcing is the process of finding people within the organization or finding or establishing companies or divisions directly linked to the organization to perform tasks inside the organization instead of having those tasks performed outside the organization. There are a variety of situations to insource a particular task, but most organizations insource to gain more control over tasks that are extremely complex or important or to eliminate some of the costs associated with outsourcing.

HRIS

A Human Resource Information System (HRIS) is a computer system designed to help human resource professionals carry out the day-to-day HR functions necessary for an organization to continue functioning normally. Most Human Resource Information Systems are designed to collect and store data related to the use of employee benefits, hiring, placement, training and evaluations of employees, payroll, and information about the work performed by the employee during a given period of time. An HRIS is designed to help an HR professional carry out all primary functions associated with HR needs, which include benefits administration, payroll, time and labor management, and HR management. An HRIS is not only designed to aid the HR department, but also helps the entire organization function effectively.

Strategic planning process

There are a variety of ways an organization can create a strategic plan, but most organizations begin by establishing future goals. These goals include primary goals established in the mission and vision statements and secondary goals that need to be accomplished to achieve primary goals. These are essential to the process because they act as the framework for the structure of the strategic plan. These goals not only help structure the plan, but also help measure progress as a whole and the overall effectiveness of a particular plan.

Once the organization has set goals, the second step is to analyze the organization and the elements in the environment. This analysis is designed to find strengths and weaknesses and to identify outside influences that may make it difficult to achieve goals. This can be assessed by using a SWOT analysis, a PEST analysis, a Porter's five forces analysis, and a variety of similar methods. Regardless of the method used, it is important that a good strategic plan takes the organization's merits, flaws, and outside influences into consideration.

Once an organization has established a set of goals, identified strengths and weaknesses, and identified the outside factors effecting achievement of goals, most organizations begin to construct the strategic plan. The goals establish objectives the plan is designed to accomplish. Strategies required to achieve those objectives are then developed. The strategies included in the first draft of the strategic plan will usually be very simple, but will become more complex as attempts are made to compensate for outside factors that may interfere with progress in addition to using strengths effectively and improving areas of weakness.

Once an organization has constructed a strategic plan from its goals taking its strengths, weaknesses, and outside environment into consideration, it is time to put the strategic plan into action. This step is often more complicated than it would appear because the strategic plan is only effective if the members of the organization follow the plan as it is written. To implement a strategic plan, each member must be informed of the plan they need to follow and they must carefully carry out that plan. If a few members of the organization attempt to take shortcuts or fail to follow the plan as expected, the entire plan may fail.

Once a strategic plan has been constructed and put into action, the organization must continually go back and evaluate the plan to make sure the plan is toward goal achievement. Even the best plan may be derailed by changes in the outside environment. The goals set at the beginning of the process will make measurement of the strategic plan possible so that changes can be made if needed. It is impossible to consider every internal and external factor that may affect the strategic plan, making it essential to identify and correct unexpected flaws as they arise.

Analysis

PEST analysis
A PEST analysis considers four groups of factors that may affect an organization. The "P" stands for political which refers to the laws, regulations, taxes, and other factors related to the local or federal

government. The "E" stands for economic, which refers to the current state of the economy as measured by statistics such as economic growth and inflation rate. The "S" stands for social, which refers to the culture and demographics of the area of operation, such as population size and growth, cultural and religious beliefs, age distribution, etc. The T" stands for technological, which refers to the invention and implementation of new technology, new regulations related to technology, new technology in use by competitors, etc.

SWOT analysis

A SWOT analysis considers four groups of factors that may affect an organization. The "S" stands for strengths, which refers to anything that will help achieve objectives. The "W" stands for weaknesses, which refers to anything that may prevent the organization from achieving its objectives. The "O" stands for opportunities, which refers to anything outside the organization that may help to achieve objectives. Finally, the "T" stands for threats, which refers to anything outside the organization that may prevent objectives from being achieved. In other words, SWOT refers to internal strengths and weaknesses, and external opportunities and threats affecting an organization.

Porter's five force analysis

A Porter's five force analysis considers five groups of factors that may affect an organization: the threat of substitute products, the threat of new competitors, existing competitive rivalry, the bargaining power of customers, and the bargaining power of suppliers. The threat of substitute products refers to new technology, products or services consumers may choose over the organization's current products or services. The threat of new competitors refers to how easy it is for new organizations to enter the market. The threat of existing competitive rivalry refers to other companies currently in the market competing with the organization and how those companies are attempting to stay competitive. The bargaining power of customers refers to the ability of customers to affect the organization's actions by refusing to buy the product or service if it is too expensive, does not live up to the customer's expectations, etc. The bargaining power of suppliers refers to the ability of suppliers to affect the organization's actions by controlling their access to raw materials, supplies, etc.

Cost/benefit analysis

A cost/benefit analysis is a decision-making strategy that examines and compares the total estimated cost and benefit of each available option. In most cases, the cost and benefit refers to financial issues, but the cost/analysis strategy can be used for any decision involving the use and acquisition of resources. It can be useful in determining which option will offer the greatest benefit. The benefits associated with a particular set of options may not be an accurate representation because the strategy is largely based on estimates.

Organizational life cycle

The organizational life cycle consists of four stages: birth, growth, maturity, and decline. The birth stage is when the organization is forming and includes all activities associated with establishing the framework such as acquiring capital, establishing values, and establishing an initial business plan. The growth stage is when the organization is expanding by increasing market share and profits, number of employees and locations, etc. The maturity stage is when expansion begins to level off and emphasis shifts to maintaining current attributes. Finally, the decline stage is when the organization begins to lose the ability to maintain its current attributes.

Risk and return

To make an educated decision regarding an investment or business venture, it is essential to consider potential risk and return. Potential risk is a measurement of the likelihood that the undertaking will offer a return rather than a loss of resources devoted to that particular undertaking. Potential return is a measurement of how much monetary value can be achieved from a particular undertaking. The higher the potential risk, the higher the potential return needs to be for that particular undertaking to be worthwhile.

ERM

Enterprise risk management (ERM) refers to a variety of techniques used to identify and minimize the effects of risks that may prevent the achievement of objectives. The process usually takes place after the organization has identified threats or opportunities related to a particular objective from a SWOT or PEST analysis. Once the threat or opportunity is identified, an assessment can be made to determine the risk. The organization can then determine the appropriate response based on the level of risk associated with the threat or opportunity.

There are four response strategies an organization can use to respond to a risk: reducing the effects of the risk, sharing the risk, avoiding the risk, or accepting the risk. Reducing the risk includes any action taken to make the risk less likely to occur or less likely to cause significant harm to the organization. Sharing the risk includes any action that transfers some of the risk to another business entity (such as by transferring the risk to an insurance company by purchasing an insurance policy). Avoiding the risk refers to discontinuing any activities associated with the risk to eliminate the risk entirely. Accepting the risk refers to monitoring the risk because the potential benefits of the opportunity outweigh the potential cost.

It is important for an HR professional to be able to manage risk effectively because a great deal of the organization's financial risk will be related to human resources. Some of the most costly risks are related to liability and legal concerns. These concerns include being held liable for the unethical, illegal, or inappropriate actions of employees, fines for not filling out and/or filing government forms correctly, etc. Since many of these risks can be controlled through careful monitoring and intelligent risk management, it is essential for an HR professional to be able to identify risks as they appear and to find ways to reduce the chance that those risks will affect the organization.

There are a variety of methods an HR professional can use to identify potential risks to the organization, but the most common method is an HR audit. An HR audit consists of a checklist, survey, or similar communication designed to assess whether a particular employee or department understands and is adhering to the policies, procedures, and regulations set by the organization. An

- 27 -

HR audit is designed to ensure each employee is adhering to all laws and regulations set by the local, state, and federal government. The format used for an HR audit will vary to adapt to the wide range of risks or to make sure that a specific risk, such as fines associated with a newly passed law, can be avoided.

Change

Change management

Change management refers to a variety of techniques used to modify a particular aspect of how the organization operates with as little harm to the organization as possible. In most cases, an organization makes these changes to adapt to changes in society or to improve operations overall. Change management is important because with a changing environment, the need to adapt is constant. It is important to adapt with as little stress as possible to allow an organization to continue function normally while changes are implemented.

Implementing change

There are three types of strategies an organization might use to implement changes: the empirical-rational strategy, the normative-reeducative strategy, and the power-coercive strategy. Choosing a strategy depends upon a variety of factors including how much the organization needs to change and what resources are available to relieve problems that may arise from the implemented changes. The decision may be determined by how much time is available to make the changes and the level of risk associated with members of the organization rejecting the change and refusing to make the necessary adjustments.

The empirical-rational strategy of managing change assumes people are ultimately interested in their own well being and, as a result, will be more likely to accept changes if they understand how they as individuals will benefit from those changes. For example, if an organization is attempting to improve its image with the public, it might offer a bonus to the employee who performs the most community service. This might encourage more employees to take part in community service projects, which may in turn improve the organization's public image.

The normative-reeducative strategy of managing change is based on the concept that peer pressure is often an effective way to bring about change in an organization. This strategy assumes that people rely heavily on social interaction and will therefore act according to societal expectations. Using this strategy, changes are introduced slowly so each individual will begin to accept the changes as social norms. For example, if an organization wants to change a particular manufacturing process, but the employees of have a process they have been using for years, new procedures might be introduced through memos, posters, and training to ease them into the new methods.

The power-coercive strategy of managing change is based on the concept that people will usually listen to authority figures and will ultimately do as they are told. This strategy works by making it clear that there are no options other than those chosen by management. In fact, under this strategy, if an individual refuses to accept the changes, the organization might punish the individual for not complying. For example, if a large grocery store must comply with a new ordinance that prohibits the sale of eggs to anyone under the age of 18 during the month of October, that grocery store may use a power-coercive strategy by informing the staff. If an employee sells eggs to a minor during October, the manager may suspend or terminate that individual.

Ethics

Business ethics is the practice of using a series of appropriate practices, procedures, and behaviors to make sure an organization functions in a socially acceptable fashion. Business ethics ensures that each individual is performing their duties in a fair, proper, and morally responsible manner. It is essential for any organization, regardless of type, to maintain a strong sense of what is appropriate and what is unacceptable. Questionable, unfair or illegal practices within an organization will risk its reputation and ability to find customers and suppliers, liability and criminal charges from unethical or unlawful practices, and maybe even its ability to do business at all.

There are a variety of ways an HR professional can establish and maintain a strong sense of ethics within an organization, but the three most effective ways include: establishing a corporate values statement, establishing a code of conduct, and making sure that each individual follows the ethical codes set by the organization through HR audits. A corporate values statement is a declaration of the basic behaviors desired of employees, including behaviors such as promoting open communication, being a team player, and treating fellow employees, customers, and other individuals with respect and dignity. A code of conduct is a series of policies, procedures, and practices that expands on the behaviors established by the values statement to define what is considered acceptable behavior and what is considered absolutely unacceptable. Finally, HR audits ensure members follow the set policies.

There are a variety of policies and procedures an HR professional might need to establish to support ethical and legal corporate governance practices including: policies to protect employees who report unethical behavior, training programs to educate managers and executives regarding legal and ethical concerns, and checklists and review systems to make sure the organization is documenting and reporting everything appropriately. Policies to protect employees that report unethical behavior might include confidentiality, the acceptance of anonymous reports, and procedures for handling managers that punish employees for reporting unethical behavior. Training programs that educate managers and executives about legal and ethical concerns might include information about sexual harassment, standards for corporate responsibility, ethical requirements for senior financial officers, and the legal concerns associated with fraud. Finally, checklists and review systems might include scheduled and unscheduled accounting audits.

Basic functions of organizations

Some of the basic types of functions an organization must typically perform to function normally include accounting functions, employee functions, financial functions, IT functions, marketing and sales functions, operating functions, and research/development functions. Accounting functions include any task that keeps track of the financial resources of the organization. Employee functions include any task related to the organization's human resources. Financial functions include any task related to earning, managing, or spending capital. IT functions include any task related to the organization's computer systems or other technology. Marketing and sales functions include any task related to the promoting, distributing, and sale of the product by considering factors such as the product itself, the price of the product, the placement or location where the product is sold, and the promotion of the product. Operating functions include any task related to the product or service the organization is attempting to sell. The research/development functions of the organization include any task related to designing new products or services.

HR professionals

HR professionals have traditionally been expected to enforce policies, but were not actively involved in policy-making and planning. However, the HR professional of today functions as an essential administrative tool, analyst, consultant, and manager. The HR professional promotes the success of the organization by helping to establish the organization's strategic plan, analyzes risks associated with the organization operations, and helps establish and enforce the policies and practices.

Important terms

The following are terms related to business and strategic management:
- Mission Statement - A mission statement is a declaration of the general purpose for which an organization has been created. It indicates the broad mission so that the reason an organization exists can be easily identified. For example, the mission statement of a hospital might be "to promote the health and well-being of the general public in order to live longer, healthier lives."
- Vision Statement - A vision statement is a declaration of the specific goals an organization wants to achieve at some point. For example, a hospital might want to become recognized as the number one health care provider in the region.
- Goal - A goal is a particular objective to be achieved at some point in the future. For example, a business might set a goal of increasing their profits for the year by 25% over the previous year.
- Business Metric - A business metric, also known as a performance metric or a key performance indicator, refers to a system of measuring a business' progress toward a goal. In most cases, a business metric is a group of statistics a company can use to determine progress in achieving a particular goal. For example, a business with the goal of increasing profits by 25% over the previous year may use profit/loss reports from the current year and compare those to the previous year to determine progress.
- Third-party vendor - A third-party vendor is an independent contractor or company providing products or services for the organization, but is not directly related to the organization. It is an outside vendor under contract to perform a service for the organization, but does not work for a division of the organization or for an organization it owns or operates. For example, a convenience store may have a contract with a soda company to deliver soda to the store and stock the store's coolers.
- Request for proposal - A request for proposal (RFP) is a written invitation sent to third-party vendors requesting bids for a specific product or service. Organizations usually issue these requests to gather information about a product or service that the organization is considering outsourcing to a third-party vendor.

Workforce Planning and Employment

Discrimination and unlawful employment practices

Discrimination refers to the process of making a decision about a particular individual or thing based on the specific traits that make the person or thing different from other individuals or things. Because the practice of discrimination is a type of decision-making, it is only illegal under certain conditions. Unlawful employment practices refer to a series of specific business actions related to hiring, training, employee compensation, and other factors related to an individual's employment prohibited by law. These practices are specifically prohibited when they prevent individuals with certain characteristics from obtaining a position, performing the duties related to a position, or receiving all of the benefits and respect from the employer normally associated with the position.

The term "discrimination" only refers to the practice of making a decision regarding a person or thing based on the characteristics of that particular person or thing, which is a practice most organizations perform legally on a daily basis. Discrimination is only unlawful if the employer's decision regarding a particular individual is based on a characteristic considered protected. For example, if an employer decides to only hire people under the age of 40, the employer is unlawfully discriminating against employees based on their age. On the other hand, if the employer decides to only hire people with a certain type of college degree and the college degree is required by law or the knowledge associated with that degree is necessary to perform the tasks related to that position, the employer is legally discriminating based on the individual's characteristics.

Disparate impact is a type of discrimination in which an employer institutes a policy that appears to be reasonable, but prevents individuals of a certain color, with certain disabilities, with a certain military status, of a certain national origin, of a certain race, of a certain religion, or individuals of a particular sex from receiving employment or any of the benefits associated with employment (such as promotions or pay). It refers to a policy that makes sense, but is actually unfair because it makes it more difficult for individuals of a certain group to receive the job or benefit. For example, a policy stating individuals applying for an office job must be at least 5'10" and weigh at least 185 pounds may create a disparate impact if it makes it more difficult for individuals belonging to one of the protected groups, such as women, to get the job. This type of discrimination was first identified by the Supreme Court in Griggs v. Duke Power Co.

Disparate treatment is a type of discrimination in which an employer deliberately treats an individual differently because of that individual's age, color, disability, military status, national origin, race, religion, and/or sex. It refers to any instance an employer uses a different set of procedures, expectations, or policies than he would normally use simply because the individual belongs to a particular group. For example, a business that required female employees to follow a strict dress code while the male employees of the business could wear whatever they like would be guilty of disparate treatment because of treating employees differently based on gender. This type of discrimination was first identified by Title VII of the Civil Rights Act.

EEOC

The Equal Opportunity Employment Commission (EEOC) was formed by Title VII of the Civil Rights Act to protect certain groups of individuals from unlawful discrimination. The EEOC is a federal agency designed to encourage equal employment opportunities, to train employers to avoid practices and policies that could cause unlawful discrimination, and to enforce the laws included in the Civil Rights Act, Age Discrimination in Employment Act, and laws included in other similar anti-discrimination legislation. The EEOC attempts to obtain settlements from employers for actions that the commission deems to be discriminatory. If the employer will not settle with the EEOC, the EEOC will continue their attempt to enforce the law by filing a lawsuit against the employer on behalf of the victim of the discrimination.

Title VII

Title VII of the Civil Rights Act, which was originally passed in 1964 and amended in 1972, 1978, and 1991, is designed to prevent unlawful discrimination in the workplace. This section of the Civil Rights Act makes it unlawful to base decisions related to aspects of an individual's employment (such as the pay or benefits) on color, national origin, race, religion, and/or sex. Title VII also makes it unlawful for an employer to discriminate against individuals that are pregnant, about to give birth, or that have any similar medical condition. Title VII of the Civil Rights Act applies to any employer that has more than 15 employees. Exceptions include religious organizations (which can choose to only hire individuals within that religion or to consider individuals of that religion for employment before individuals of other religions), and Indian reservations (which can choose to hire or consider Indians living on or near a reservation for employment before other individuals).

ADEA

The Age Discrimination in Employment Act (ADEA), which was originally passed in 1967 and then later amended in 1991, is designed to prevent discrimination against individuals over the age of 39. This act makes it unlawful to base decisions related to an individual's employment (such as pay or benefits) on the age of the individual if that individual is at least 40 years old. This act applies to any business, employment agency, labor organization, and state or local government agency with more than 20 employees. Exceptions include individuals age 40 or over who do not meet the occupational qualifications required to perform the tasks reasonably necessary to the business' operations, termination due to reasonable cause, employment of firefighters or police officers, retirement of employees with executive positions or tenured educators under certain conditions.

Under the Age Discrimination in Employment Act, any individual may waive the right to protection from age discrimination by signing a waiver of rights. To be legal, the waiver must be written in a clear and concise manner and state that the individual should consult with an attorney prior to signing the waiver. Secondly, the employee must be allowed at least 21 days to consider the terms of the waiver and at least 7 days to change his or her mind and terminate the waiver after signing. Finally, the waiver must offer consideration such as pay or benefits in addition to anything the individual would normally receive.

Under the Age Discrimination in Employment Act, early retirement or incentive programs encouraging individuals to leave the organization, must meet certain requirements. First, the waiver must be written in a clear and concise manner, must state that the individual should consult with an attorney prior to signing the waiver, must allow the individual at least 45 days to consider the terms of the waiver, and must allow the individual to have at least 7 days to change his or her mind after signing. The employee must be informed of eligibility factors, time limits associated with the program, and the job titles and ages of each person chosen who is eligible and the ages of each person ineligible or has not been chosen to take part in the program.

ADA

The Americans with Disabilities Act (ADA), which was passed in 1990, is designed to prevent discrimination against individuals with disabilities. This act makes it unlawful to base decisions related to aspects of an individual's employment (such as pay or benefits) on whether or not the individual is disabled. This act specifically requires any business, employment agency, or labor organization with more than 15 employees to find or create a position the disabled individual will be able to perform as long as creating that position will not cause the business significant financial or operational harm. This act also requires the business, employment agency, or labor organization to ensure the disabled individual has access to his or her place of employment unless making these changes will cause the business significant harm.

CRA of 1991

The Civil Rights Act (CRA) of 1991 was designed to perform four primary functions. The first function is to declare specific rights victims of discrimination may use to remedy the effects of discrimination. The second function of the CRA is to acknowledge and define the type of discrimination known as disparate impact. The third function of the CRA is to offer specific regulations and guidelines related to disparate impact cases. Finally, the fourth function is to expand on the discrimination laws and regulations that were established before the Civil Rights Act of 1991 to offer more protection against discrimination. It was primarily included to strengthen some of the equal opportunity laws not offering enough protection due to rulings made by the Supreme Court.

The Civil Rights Act of 1991 made a number of changes to Title VII of the Civil Rights Act of 1964 including expanding the protection offered by Title VII to cover congressional employees, expanding the protection offered by Title VII to cover foreign locations owned and/or operated by American businesses, and creating a sliding scale for the maximum amount of damages for which a victim of discrimination could sue. The Civil Rights Act of 1991 also granted individuals or organizations accused of discrimination the right to a jury trial if a civil suit is brought against that individual or organization, placed the burden of proof for disparate impact cases on the victim of discrimination, and granted individuals or organizations accused of discrimination the right to prove that a specific action or policy was necessary to the operation of the business and use that proof as a legal defense against accusations of disparate impact. The Civil Rights Act of 1991 also set guidelines defining specific actions that should be considered unlawful discrimination.

Rehabilitation Act of 1973

The Rehabilitation Act of 1973 is similar to the Americans with Disabilities Act (ADA) in that the Rehabilitation Act is designed to prevent discrimination against individuals with disabilities. However, the ADA expands the protections granted by the Rehabilitation Act which was only designed to prevent discrimination against individuals with disabilities if those individuals were seeking employment in federal agencies or with federal contractors that earned more than $10,000 a year from government contracts. Employers were not required under the Rehabilitation Act to make the organization's facilities accessible to individuals with disabilities so there was no legal remedy for an individual that was employed, but was unable to access his or her place of employment.

VEVRAA

The Vietnam Era Veteran's Readjustment Assistance Act (VEVRAA) is designed to prevent discrimination against veterans. This act makes it unlawful for federal contractors or subcontractors with $25,000 or more in federal contracts or subcontracts to base employment decisions (such as pay or benefits) on the fact that the individual is a veteran. It also requires federal contractors or subcontractors meeting these requirements to list open positions with state employment agencies and requires these employers to institute affirmative action plans for veterans. However, in order for this act to apply, the veteran must have served for more than 180 days with at least part of that time occurring between August 5th, 1964 and May 7th, 1975, or the veteran must have a disability or group of disabilities that are rated at 10 percent or more and be eligible for compensation from the Department of Veteran Affairs, or the veteran must have served on active duty for a conflict with an authorized campaign badge.

IRCA

The Immigration Reform and Control Act (IRCA) is designed to prevent discrimination based on nationality. This act makes it unlawful for an employer to base employment decisions (such as pay or benefits) on that individual's country of origin or citizenship status as long as the individual can legally work within the United States. This act also makes it unlawful for an organization to intentionally hire individuals that cannot legally work in the United States and requires the completion of the I-9 form for all new employees. This act specifically requires the employer to obtain proof of the employee's eligibility to work in the United States for the I-9 form, but the employee must be allowed to provide any document or combination of documents considered acceptable by the IRCA.

Discrimination claims and lawsuits

To file a discrimination claim, the claim must be made within a certain length of time from the time that the specific discriminatory act occurs. If the individual is filing in a state with an equal employment opportunity enforcement agency, the claim must be filed within 300 days of the incident. If the individual is filing in a state that does not have an equal employment opportunity enforcement agency, the claim must be filed within 180 days of the incident. If the discrimination claim is not filed within the appropriate time limit, the Equal Employment Opportunity Commission (EEOC) will not investigate the claim.

To file a discrimination lawsuit, a discrimination claim must be filed and notification received from the Equal Employment Opportunity Commission (EEOC). If the EEOC establishes enough evidence to prove unlawful discrimination, the EEOC will attempt to reach a settlement. If the EEOC cannot reach a settlement, they may file a lawsuit on the victim's behalf. If the EEOC determines there is not enough evidence the individual has 90 days to file suit. Otherwise the individual forfeits the right to file any lawsuit related to that specific act of discrimination.

The Civil Rights Act of 1991 establishes a sliding scale for the total amount of compensatory and punitive damages an individual can receive from a discrimination suit. This sliding scale is based on the number of employees. The maximum amount an individual can be awarded increases as the size of the organization increases. If the individual is suing an organization with more than 15, but less than 101 employees, the maximum the individual can receive is $50,000. If the individual is suing an organization with more than a 100 employees, but less than 201 employees, the maximum the individual can receive is $100,000. If the individual is suing an organization with more than 200 employees, but less than 501 employees, the maximum the individual can receives is $200,000. Finally, if the individual is suing an organization with more than 500 employees, the maximum the individual can receive is $300,000. However, it is important to note that these limits **only** apply to compensatory and punitive damages.

Meritor Savings Bank v. Vinson

The Supreme Court case known as Meritor Savings Bank v. Vinson recognized sexual harassment as a form of unlawful discrimination. The case was brought against Meritor Savings Bank by Mechelle Vinson because the bank's vice president had created a hostile work environment through a series of repeated unwelcome sexual advances and acts. Prior to this case, the protections offered by Title VII of the Civil Rights Act of 1964 for discrimination based on sex had been related solely to economic or other tangible discrimination. However, Title VII was designed to prevent all types of "disparate treatment" which cause a hostile work environment for a member of a protected class constitute a form of unlawful discrimination.

UGESP

The Uniform Guidelines on Employee Selection Procedures (UGESP), which were passed in 1978, are actually a collection of principles, techniques, and procedures designed to help employers comply with Federal anti-discrimination laws. The primary purpose of these guidelines is to define the specific types of procedures that may cause disparate impact and are considered illegal. The UGESP relates to unfair procedures, which make it much less likely that an individual belonging to a protected class would be able to receive a particular position.

Executive orders

An executive order is a written declaration made by the President of the United States establishing a policy for enforcing existing legislation. Executive orders are legally binding and are treated as law if the order remains in the Federal Registry for more than 30 days. Executive order 11246, which was published to the Federal Registry in 1965 states that federal contractors are not only required to avoid employment discrimination, but are also required to take steps to ensure equal opportunities are available to individuals belonging to protected classes. This executive order established the concept of affirmative action and required federal contractors with more than $10,000 in government contracts during a single year to implement affirmative action plans and federal contractors with $50,000 or more in contracts and 50 or more employees to file written affirmative action plans with the Office of Federal Contract Compliance Programs (OFCCP.)

Originally, Executive Order (EO) 11246 only applied to employment discrimination based on an individual's color, national origin, race, or religion. However, EO 11375, EO 11478, EO 13152, and EO 13279 amended the policy and changed the groups that were covered. EO 11375 made it unlawful to discriminate based on sex; EO 11478 made it unlawful to discriminate based on disabilities or age if that individual is over age 40; EO 13152 made it unlawful to base discrimination on parental status; and EO 13279 excluded federal contractors who were religious or community organizations providing services to the community from the need to adhere to the policies.

AAPs

Written Affirmative Action Plans (AAP) were first established by Executive Order 11246. The main purpose of an AAP, as established by a revision to 41 CFR Part 60-2 made in late 2000, requires the establishment of a series of goals related to equal employment opportunities. An AAP includes a list of action-oriented programs, an availability analysis of employees from protected classes, a section that designates the individual responsible for the organization's AAP, a job group analysis, an organizational profile, placement goals, a system for internal audits and reports related to analyzing barriers to equal employment opportunities, and a utilization/incumbency analysis of the number of protected individuals employed by the company compared to the number of protected individuals available.

The availability analysis of an Affirmative Action Plan (AAP) includes information related to the number of individuals belonging to a protected class within a certain area that could be hired to fill a particular type of position. It is a report of the estimated number of individuals for one of the protected classes externally available through the hiring process or internally available for a particular type of job from another department within the organization. The job group analysis of an AAP includes information related to the structure of job groups within the organization. Each job title is separated into groups of related jobs and then determines the number of employees within each group. The report must also determine the appropriate Equal Employment Opportunity category code associated with each job group.

The utilization analysis of an Affirmative Action Plan (AAP), also referred to as an incumbency analysis, includes information comparing the number of available individuals belonging to a protected class within a certain area with the number of individuals belonging to a protected class actually hired for a particular group of jobs. This report usually consists of a chart showing the percentage of the local labor pool in a protected class within each job group compared with employees actually hired. The analysis of equal employment opportunity barriers of an AAP determines the monitoring procedures in place to identify the effectiveness of affirmative action plans. It establishes the specific system of internal audits and reports. This ensures problems are continually identified and eliminated.

The placement goals section of an Affirmative Action Plan (AAP) is a list of specific objectives to improve problems identified by the AAP by the various analyses, audits, or reports conducted. Usually, placement goals are necessary if the utilization/incumbency analysis indicates that the percentage of individuals employed by belonging to a specific protected class is less than 80% of the percentage belonging to the group of individuals with the highest percentage. For example, an organization that had 300 white applicants and hired 100 white employees and had 200 African-American applicants and hired 50 African-American employees would have hired 33% (100/300) of the white employees available and 25% (50/200) of the African American employees available. This organization would need to set placement goals for the organization because 25% is not equal to 80% or 4/5 of 33% (33% * 80% = 26.6%).

The action-oriented programs section of an Affirmative Action Plan (AAP) should establish the specific procedures, policies, and plans the organization intends to use to meet placement goals or to fix problems identified by internal audits or reports. The information included in this section must provide a detailed explanation of the procedural plans for making changes to the employment system and provide specific dates deadlines for procedural implementation and progress. It is also essential that the procedures and plans included are different from plans introduced in previous years that have failed to deliver desired results.

The designation of responsibility section of an Affirmative Action Plan (AAP) is a list of names and titles of managers and HR professionals responsible for AAP implementation, monitoring, and for making corrections. It is also important in identifying which professionals will perform each task. The organizational profile section of an AAP expands the information included in the job group analysis. It contains information about the pay assigned to each job title within a specific job group, the number of males and females holding each job title, and the number of individuals of each ethnicity holding each job title. The primary purpose of this section is to identify areas of large differences in pay between people of different races or gender.

Workforce planning

Because the specific skills and knowledge needed to perform tasks vary from organization to organization, from department to department, and from position to position, workforce planning is essential. The needs of an organization can change as size or environment changes, making it important to identify available human resources and human resources for future needs.

Some of the most common activities an organization might perform in the workforce planning process include conducting staffing forecasts, establishing staffing goals and objectives, conducting job analyses, and establishing plans to meet staffing goals and objectives. Many organizations begin by conducting a staffing forecast, which refers to any analysis determining how staffing needs might change. Once an organization has conducted a staffing forecast, the organization may set specific staffing goals and objectives describing current and future positions to fill. After staffing goals and objectives are established, each position is analyzed to determine specific qualifications needed. Finally, a plan is established to find and hire individuals to fill these positions.

Forecasting methods

The two main types of forecasting methods an organization might use to evaluate changing labor needs are qualitative forecasting methods and quantitative forecasting methods. Qualitative forecasting methods include any forecasting method based on the opinions or analyses of managers or experts in the industry. Quantitative forecasting methods are based on actual data, such as past trends or employee to output ratios. The difference in the two types is qualitative is based on knowledge and opinion and quantitative is based on statistics or mathematical data.

The most common qualitative forecasting methods include management forecasts and a variety of techniques associated with expert forecasting. Management forecasts determine future staffing needs by asking managers of each department to discuss staffing needs at a meeting or by submitting reports. Expert forecasting methods (such as the Delphi method) seek the opinion of experts outside the organization. This allows information to be obtained about the effects of changes in the industry or changes from a variety of sources. That information is then formed into a report about possible changes in staffing needs.

Some of the most common quantitative forecasting methods include historical ratios analyses, trend analyses, turnover analyses and probability models. A ratio analysis is a type of analysis comparing current employment ratios (such as the number of employees required to produce a certain number of products) with past ratios to determine staffing needs might change in the future. Trend analyses compare a single current employment variable (such as the number of employees) with a past employment variable rather than comparing two ratios. Turnover analyses examine the rate employees leave the organization during a given period compared to previous turnover rates. Probability models allow the organization to chart and predict data related to changes in the organization.

The two most important factors to consider when deciding which forecasting method to use are how far in the future the organization is attempting to plan and if the organization needs to change at a steady rate. Qualitative methods are usually effective for short-term forecasts or for constantly changing staffing needs and quantitative methods are more effective for long-term forecasts in organizations that have staffing needs that change at a steady rate. Most organizations need both short-term and long-term forecasts.

Job analysis

A job analysis is an essential part of any workforce planning process because it identifies specific skills and knowledge required to meet staffing goals and objectives. It also identifies the specific skills and qualifications required to meet the strategic goals and objectives set for the organization as a whole. A job analysis allows the organization to not only identify which tasks need to be performed, but also breaks those tasks into specific skills, traits, and knowledge that would qualify an individual to perform each task appropriately.

The three main components an organization identifies during a job analysis include job descriptions, job competencies, and job specifications. A job description is a detailed breakdown of all tasks, specific skills and knowledge needed for a particular position. Job competencies are a detailed list of all broad skills and traits (such as leadership ability) needed for a particular position. Job specifications are detailed descriptions of all specific qualifications (such as experience or education) an individual must have to perform the task.

Recruiting

The recruiting process, which refers to the procedures and strategies used to encourage potential candidates to seek employment with the organization, is an essential part of any organization's staffing plan. Without a suitable labor pool, it is impossible for an organization to meet its staffing goals and objectives. Recruiting strategies help develop and find qualified candidates to fill each position.

The three main ways an organization recruits potential employees include external recruiting, internal recruiting, and alternative recruiting. External recruiting attempts to encourage individuals from outside to seek employment with the organization. This type of recruiting usually consists of strategies that stress the advantages of working for the organization. Internal recruiting attempts to encourage individuals from within to seek transfers or promotions into vacant positions the organization needs to fill. Alternative recruiting refers to the process of finding interns, telecommuters, or temps to perform specific tasks.

Most external recruiting strategies rely on advertising which appeals to potential candidates by promoting the organization's benefits (pay, insurance, product discounts) and improving the organization's image (with the public and employees). These factors will make it easier to find skilled employees.

There are several recruiting strategies an organization might use to find qualified individuals from within the organization to fill vacant positions, but some of the most common strategies include internal job announcements, job bidding, and promotion/succession plans. Internal job announcements are job postings only available to individuals within the organization or available before they are made available to the general public. Internal job announcements are usually posted as new positions become available. Job bidding is a process in which employees inform the organization of their interest in transferring to another position regardless of the availability of that position. A promotion/succession plan strategy is a chart or list detailing each employee, their skills and training, and the specific positions they are qualified to fill. These positions are filled by offering promotions or additional training to these qualified individuals.

Screening tools

Because of the large number of candidates and the small number of available positions, screening tools are essential. Eliminating unqualified candidates saves money and time and focuses resources on those individuals most suited for each position. The screening tools most commonly used include employment applications, resumes, and interviews. Employment applications include any form designed by an employer requiring an individual to give personal information, previous experience, education, etc. Resumes are usually one to two pages and list experience, education, and references qualifying an individual for a particular position. Resumes are not usually a pre-made form to be filled out, but rather a document designed and written by the individual seeking employment. Interviews used for screening are meetings with an applicant designed to determine whether an individual should be considered for a position.

There are three main types of employment applications commonly used during an organization's hiring process: general employment applications, job-specific employment applications, and weighted employment applications. The most common form is the general employment application which requests information related to employment history, education, and overall background. A job-specific employment application is used by organizations needing to fill a large number of similar positions or hire individuals for similar positions on a regular basis. Job-specific employment applications are forms requesting information directly related to the qualifications necessary to perform the job. Weighted employment applications are forms requesting answers to questions or information related to specific requirements necessary to perform the duties associated with the position. Each requirement is then assigned a weight based on its importance to the position.

The two common types of general employment applications are the short-form and long-form employment applications. A short-form application consists of a pre-made form designed to obtain general information. A short-form application is for positions not requiring a large number of specialized skills or for individuals within the organization attempting to change positions. A long-form application is a pre-made form designed to obtain a more in-depth idea of an individual's skills or knowledge. A long-form application is the most commonly used general employment application.

Selection tools

During the hiring process, the selection tools most commonly used include interviews, pre-employment tests, and realistic job previews. Interviews (at the selection stage of the hiring process) refer to any meeting with an applicant designed to determine if an individual should receive the position. Pre-employment tests include any written examination administered prior to hiring an employee designed to evaluate the applicant's specific skills and knowledge. A realistic job preview (RJP) refers to any activity that helps give the applicant an idea of the specific day-to-day tasks and responsibilities they will need to perform, including activities such as watching videos about the organization, observing current employees, or presentations of the job being performed.

Selection tools are an essential part of an organization's hiring process because the goal is to find groups of acceptable employees and then choose the best candidate from that group. However, even if an organization has located a suitable group of potential employees, it can be extremely difficult for an interviewer to separate the most qualified individual from the rest of the group based on applications and resumes alone. As a result, it is necessary to have a set of well-defined selection tools and methods that are both valid and reliable.

Interviews
The two main styles of interviewing used during a selection interview are directive and nondirective. The directive style of interviewing refers to an interview that is directed or controlled by the interviewer. They are carefully planned prior to the interview to include a list of specific questions to ask. The interviewer will make every effort to ask all of the questions included on the list without being distracted by the applicant. Although the interviewer using the

nondirective style may have a short list of questions prepared to start the discussion, there is more interest in interacting with the applicant than there is in covering specific topics.

Two of the most common types of selection interviews include behavioral interviews and panel interviews. In a behavioral interview, the applicant is asked questions about how they handled situations in the past. These questions give the applicant an opportunity to detail their application of skills and knowledge in the past, which helps give the interviewer insight into how they might handle future situations. A single applicant is interviewed by a group in the panel interview. Panel interviews are used so several managers, team members, or HR professionals can evaluate the candidate and decide as a group whether the candidate is suited for the position.

The main advantage of an interview during the hiring process is that it allows the organization to personally evaluate the extent of an individual's skills and knowledge related to a particular field. A resume or application will list the individual's work experience, education, etc., but these documents are not necessarily indications of job performance or ability. Because they are designed to help the applicant present themselves well, they are usually limited to gathering basic information. A personal interview, (one-to-one or group-to-one) allows for more demonstration of the individual's actual abilities.

There are two main disadvantages associated with a selection interview. First, it can be heavily affected by the interviewer's own biases. Regardless of how much experience or training an interviewer has, preconceived ideas of a particular candidate or a particular type of candidate can influence the evaluation. Secondly, even the best planned interview can be rendered useless when intelligent applicants, wanting to cast themselves in the best possible light, control the interview. This is a problem for a directive interviewer attempting to assess the applicant's skills. When the interviewer does not ask the right questions, the applicant may appear to be a magnificent candidate even though the necessary skills to perform the job are absent.

Pre-employment tests
Two of the most common types of pre-employment tests are aptitude tests and in-box tests. An aptitude test is an examination designed to determine if an individual has the basic knowledge to perform the tasks associated with a particular position. For example, an aptitude test for a bank teller might consist of a series of basic math problems related to specific banking activities (such as determining an account balance after several deposits and withdrawals). In an in-box test, the individual must determine the appropriate way to handle particular problems. For example, a head bank teller might identify the appropriate manner to handle a check deposited into the wrong account.

The two main advantages associated with pre-employment tests are: they allow the organization to have more control over the information gathered and they make it easier to gather information in a consistent way. Pre-employment tests comprise pre-made questions assessing the individual's ability to use specific skills and areas of knowledge, which helps diminish the false appearance of an applicant's qualifications. Pre-employment tests provide consistent results as long as each applicant takes the exam under the same conditions.

There are several disadvantages associated with using a pre-employment test. First, it is easy to unintentionally cause a disparate impact to a protected class if questions are not relevant to the position for which the individual is applying. A series of poorly worded or irrelevant questions may make it more difficult for a particular group of people to get the job, which may make the organization legally liable. Secondly, pre-employment tests do not allow for flexibility because the same questions are asked of every applicant. An interviewer is able to ask questions related to information an applicant's resume while a pre-employment test cannot.

Validity of tools

One reason valid and reliable screening tools are important is to avoid unintentionally causing a disparate impact to a particular group of individuals because of hiring procedures examining qualifications not necessarily related to the actual position. Since disparate impact is unlawful discrimination, an organization using questionable screening procedures may unintentionally open itself to liability. Another reason valid and reliable screening tools are important is to ensure the employee hired for a position is suitable. When a screening procedure does not actually relate to the position or provides inconsistent information, highly qualified candidates might be eliminated.

To ensure a particular screening process is valid and reliable, there should be well-defined information about the applicant relevant to the position. If the procedure used to gather information from the applicant does not actually assess the basic qualifications or the information is not relevant to the specific position being applied for, the screening process is probably inaccurate or unfair. A valid screening tool should provide information that is well-defined, relevant, and job-related.

The three main types of validity an HR professional may need to evaluate to determine if a screening or selection tool is valid are construct validity, content validity, and criterion validity. Construct validity assesses the specific traits shown to indicate success for a particular position. It must test for specific characteristics shown to be indicators of job performance. Conduct validity assesses the skills and knowledge necessary to perform the tasks associated with a particular position. Criterion validity is used to predict how an individual will behave in the work place based on written or verbal test scores.

The two types of criterion validity an HR professional may evaluate to determine if a screening or selection tool is valid are concurrent and predictive validity. Concurrent validity indicates that the individual currently possesses the desired trait or will behave in the desired fashion. For example, a test might be considered valid if test scores indicate the individual remains calm in stressful situations, as indicated by a stressful situation the organization places the individual into at the time of the test. Predictive validity indicates that the individual will possess the desired trait or will behave in the desired fashion at some point in the future.

Common recruiting places

Some of the places organizations commonly use to find new employees include job listings and advertisements, career fairs and employment-related organizations/centers, and word-of-mouth recruiting. Job listings and advertisements are found in magazines, newspapers, on the organization's website, on employment websites, etc. Career fairs and employment-related organizations/centers are career placement offices, employment agencies, job fairs, labor unions, open houses, professional organizations, unemployment offices, and universities. Word-of-mouth recruiting is through employee referrals and suggestions made by former employees.

Unusual recruiting sources

Many organizations will target their outside recruiting efforts in places such as job listings, career fairs, and employment offices to increase the number of possible candidates for available positions. However, when these do not provide the adequate number of candidates, more unusual sources may need to be pursued. Some of these are passing out fliers, looking for employees in religious organizations, using employees from prison work programs, looking for individuals leaving vendors and suppliers who may make good employees, and offering sign-on bonuses.

References

Reference checks are an important part of any organization's hiring process for a couple of reasons. First, reference checks verify individuals have the skills and knowledge necessary to perform the position for which they are being hired. The second reason is that they allow an organization to protect itself from lawsuits and damage to the operations or reputation from employees who are inept. References may identify past problems that may not show up on a resume or application.

The two main types of references an organization would normally need to check are educational and employment. Educational references are certifications, degrees, diplomas, professional licenses, scholarly awards, or other documents used to prove the individual's knowledge. Universities or certification organizations may provide specific information about performance such as grades, but most educational reference checks are only used to verify education and the dates each degree, certification, or license was earned. Employment references refer to previous employers, co-workers, or customers who can verify experience. An organization will usually seek on-the-job performance information from previous employers and co-workers in addition to position, pay, and length of employment.

There are many types of reference checks an organization might use, but two less common are financial and driving history checks. Financial reference checks request information about credit history to gain an understanding of how the individual handles money, usually requested only for positions in which the individual will be handling money on the job. Driving history checks gain information about the individual's driving record in order to ensure safe driving capability, usually only when driving is required for the job.

Criminal records

It is important to check criminal records because individuals causing problems in the past will often cause problems in the future, which could lead to damage or liability to an organization. Criminal records will indicate if the individual has been convicted of a crime so that a determination can be made if those crimes relate to the position. In many cases the crime the individual committed may not be relevant to how the individual will perform in a particular position. However a history of violent crimes, theft, or substance abuse may make hiring the individual prohibitive.

Employee Polygraph Protection Act of 1988

The Employee Polygraph Protection Act of 1988 was designed to protect individuals seeking employment from being required to submit to polygraph tests. This act specifically forbids private employers from basing hiring decisions on polygraph tests unless the individual is seeking a position that involves pharmaceuticals, working in an armored car or as a security officer. This act does not apply to any government agency or federal contractor or subcontractor with FBI, national defense, or national security contracts. If an employer requires a polygraph test and the position is not related to one of these areas, fines are up to $10,000.

Employee concerns

Job offers
The method an organization uses to offer a position to an individual can vary from state to state. In many states, there are "employment-at-will" laws that allow both the organization and the employee to terminate the employment agreement at any time for any reason. An organization can usually offer employment by making a verbal offer and the individual can choose to accept that offer or decline it without signing a formal contract. However, most organizations, regardless of the state, will use written offer letters or employment contracts in addition to verbal offers to clearly state the duties and benefits associated with the position.

Medical examinations and drug tests
An organization may require employees to receive medical examinations and/or drug tests before they begin work to determine physical ability to perform the job safely. Certain occupations (such as warehouse and police work) require heavy lifting and the ability to perform strenuous activity for extended periods. Medical examinations are only used for positions with specific physical requirements and are administered to everyone in a similar position equally to avoid causing a disparate impact. Drug tests can legally be administered for any position because of the increased risk of accidents among individuals abusing a substance.

Employment contracts
Each organization will tailor employment contracts to the specific needs of the organization. However, all employment contracts should include the specific tasks and responsibilities the individual will be expected to perform, start date and duration of contract, compensation and benefits, and voided contract termination conditions. Contact information, nondisclosure agreements, and non-solicitation agreements preventing the individual from trying to convince customers or suppliers to continue buying from or selling to the individual after the contract has elapsed may also be helpful.

Employee orientation
An employee orientation, also known as an on-boarding program, is a program designed to help employees become effective members of the organization. The first step is to ensure resources are available necessary to job performance. Tools and workspace should be set up before the employee's first day on the job in addition to a formal explanation regarding the organization's mission, objectives, and values. The individual's specific position and department can then be addressed by introducing co-workers and supervisors, showing the individual around the facilities, explaining the department's rules, guidelines, and goals, and by identifying places to find help.

Employee retention programs
An employee retention program is a set of policies, procedures, and practices designed to encourage employees to stay with a particular organization. These programs can be an essential part of a staffing strategy by decreasing constant changes caused by employees seeking better benefits or higher pay. Keeping abreast of these issues is especially important for individuals in positions that require specific skills and are therefore difficult and costly to replace. Employee retention programs offering extra benefits or compensation (such as extra vacation time, extra pay, and bonuses) help the organization retain staff and function effectively.

Employment termination

The two main types of employment termination are voluntary and involuntary. Voluntary termination is employment that is terminated by the choice of the employee. Involuntary termination is employment the organization ends regardless of whether the employee wishes to stay or not. Involuntary terminations are usually used when the employee has been performing poorly or staffing needs have changed.

Examples of voluntary employment termination are: finding work elsewhere, unhappiness with the organization, health problems, desire for further education, and retirement. The two main types of involuntary terminations are layoffs and performance-related terminations. Layoffs usually occur because the organization is facing internal or environmental problems that can only be addressed in this way. Performance-related terminations usually occur when an employee has failed to meet expectations.

Exit interviews

An exit interview is a written or verbal survey used to gauge an individual's opinion of the overall effectiveness of each part of the staffing strategy. They give a better idea of the screening process, the selection process, the training programs, etc. and work to maintain staffing needs. These interviews can also be an important part of an employment termination process because they are informative of the employment process functions from the employee's point of view. Most employees are reluctant to express criticism while employed by the organization, making a written survey or an interview when leaving the company a more effective measurement of staffing strategies.

WARNA

The Worker Adjustment and Retraining Act (WARNA), which was passed in 1988, is designed to ensure employees have an opportunity to seek other employment before their employment is terminated as part of a mass layoff or plant closing. This act requires employers with 100 or more full-time employees to notify each employee or their union representatives in writing of a pending mass layoff or plant closing at least 60 days prior to the actual event. It also applies to employers with 100 or more employees that work either full or part time if those employees work for a total of 4000 hours or more an average workweek. WARNA does not apply to plant closings or mass layoffs that are a result of a national disaster or are the result of unforeseeable business circumstances and WARNA does not apply to plant closings if there is a reasonable expectation they will receive funding to keep the plant open.

A mass layoff as identified by WARNA is an event in which a plant does not actually close, but a large number of employees lose their employment due to the event. A mass layoff is considered such if during a 90-day period 500 or more employees, or 50 or more employees if those employees make up 33% or more of the organization's workforce, will lose their jobs permanently, lose their jobs for more than six months, or receive at least a 51% reduction in the number of hours they are allowed to work per month for six months or more. Employees who have worked for the organization for less than 6 months in the past year and employees who work less than 20 hours a week are not included for the purpose of determining if a layoff should be considered a mass layoff.

A plant closing is identified by the WARNA as an event in which an organization closes a single facility or a group of facilities located at the same site and a large number of employees lose their employment as a result. According to WARNA, an organization must give notice 60 days prior to the time a plant will be closed permanently, or temporarily if 50 or more employees will lose their

- 45 -

jobs permanently, lost their jobs for more than six months, or receive at least a 51% reduction in the number of hours they are allowed to work per month for six months or more if the organization decides to relocate the individual to another facility or site. However, employees who have worked for the organization for less than 6 months in the past year and employees that work less than 20 hours a week should not be included for the purposes of determining if the organization is required to give notice.

Human Resource Development

Human resource development

Human resource development, which is also referred to as talent development, is the process an organization uses to modify the behavior, skills, and knowledge of the employees to achieve goals. It describes all practices, procedures, and policies used to ensure employees are able to perform duties and responsibilities effectively.

The three main types of development usually associated with human resource development are career development, learning and development, and organization development. Career development includes any activity related to an employee's professional progress within an organization (such as encouraging individuals to seek promotions for which they may be well suited.) Learning and development, which is more commonly referred to as training, is related to teaching an employee the specific skills and knowledge required to effectively perform the tasks associated with his or her position. Organization development includes any activity that helps establish the system of methods and tools allowing employees to carry out their duties and responsibilities effectively (i.e. the installation of a new computer system allowing employees to complete certain tasks more efficiently).

Copyright Act of 1976

The Copyright Act of 1976 is designed to prevent individuals from stealing original works or claiming original works as their own. This act specifically prohibits any individual other than the copyright holder from creating works based on the original work, duplicating the original work, reproducing the original work, selling or renting copies of the original work, and performing or displaying an original work in any format without the expressed permission of the copyright holder. The protections offered by the Copyright Act apply to any original work in a tangible form and therefore includes any written, musical, or visual work such as a book or screenplay, a written or recorded song, or a movie. In most cases, these protections apply to the original author of the work considered to be the copyright holder.

In most cases, the original creator of a work is considered to be the copyright holder under the regulations set by the Copyright Act of 1976. However, there are two situations another individual or organization may hold the copyright. The first situation is when an employee creates an original work for a specific organization. In this case, the organization employing the individual is automatically assigned the copyright to the work because the individual was paid to create the work. The second situation is when an organization hires an independent individual specifically for the purpose of creating that work. In this case, the organization hiring the individual to create the work is automatically assigned the copyright because the independent individual was paid to create the work.

Public domain

Public domain is a work with no official copyright holder; therefore any individual can use the work without permission. There are two ways a work becomes public domain. The first way is that the original copyright expires. A copyright is only valid for 70 years after the death of the work's original author or for 95 years from the first publication or 120 years from the creation of the work if the work was commissioned by another individual or organization. The second way is that the work was created by a federal agency, which is automatically considered to be public domain.

Fair use

The legal concept of fair use establishes the conditions a copyrighted work may be used without permission. However, there are certain broad requirements for the use of a copyrighted work must meet to be considered fair use. First, only a limited portion of the original work may be used care must be taken to have no significant impact on the market value of the original work. Second, the selected portion of the original work must be used to critique or comment on the work or for news-related or teaching purposes, and should generally be used for educational or nonprofit uses.

U.S. Patent Act

The U.S. Patent Act is designed to prevent individuals from stealing inventions and/or claiming inventions created by other individuals as their own. This act specifically prohibits any individual other than the patent holder from producing the invention, using the invention, offering the invention to other individuals, or selling the invention unless the individual receives permission from the patent holder. The protections granted by the U.S. Patent Act only apply to inventions within the United States or to inventions entering the United States. This act does not apply to actions taken in other countries unless those actions result in the invention entering the United States. Although this act grants the patent holder the right to prevent other individuals from producing, using, offering, or selling the invention, it does not offer any specific recourse for handling patent infringement.

Patent types

The three types of patents an individual or organization may hold in the United States are design, plant, and utility patents. Design patents are patents protect new, original, and ornamental designs related to the manufacturing of a specific item. They are valid for 14 years from the date the patent is filed. Plant patents protect new types of asexually reproducing plants an individual or organization has created or discovered. Plant patents are valid for 20 years from the date that the patent is filed. Utility patents protect new or improved machinery, processes, and products. Utility patents are valid for 20 years from the date the patent is filed.

ADDIE Model

The ADDIE Model is a set of instructional design guidelines commonly used by organizations to develop human resource development (HRD) programs. This model consists of five separate steps and each step is identified by one of the letters in the term "ADDIE." "A" represents the Analysis step, the first "D" represents the Design step, the second "D" represents the Development step, the "I" represents the Implementation step, and the "E" represents the Evaluation step. Each step of the model establishes a basic set of guidelines and procedures an individual or organization can follow to develop a training or instructional program piece by piece. This procedure is commonly used in human resource development because it is a simple, but effective way of creating a training program. The ADDIE model can also be applied to a variety of fields and is not limited to training programs.

Analysis is the first step described by the ADDIE Model. The problem to solve is defined in detail and specific goals and objectives (along with the knowledge, skills and abilities required) are identified. The process is usually started by asking questions about why the program is being developed, will it be used to improve performance or eliminate performance problems, etc.

Design is the second step described by the ADDIE Model. In this step, a plan is designed to achieve the goals and objectives set forth in the analysis phase. A series of documents is created describing strategies to use to solve the problem, improve overall performance, etc. Strategies must be identified which will provide the knowledge, skills, and abilities necessary to achieve the goal.

Development is the third step described by the ADDIE Model. In this step, a series of tools (activities, exercise, handouts, etc.) are developed to carry out strategies identified during the design step. Instructional guides are also developed which will help each skill trainer understand the procedure for teaching specific information employees need to know.
Implementation is the fourth step described by the ADDIE Model. In this step, the materials created during the development stage are put into action. Most organizations will begin this phase by testing through a pilot program to allow problems to be identified and changed before the program is implemented. The program is put into action once the program is functioning as expected.

Evaluation is the fifth and final step described by the ADDIE Model. Although evaluation occurs as adjustments are made throughout the model, this step refers to an ongoing evaluation of the results of the program. Determinations are made regarding the achievement of goals and if additional programs need to be added.

Needs analysis

It is important for an organization to perform a needs analysis before designing a training program for several different reasons. First, an organization can accurately identify problems. Second, even if a particular problem is known prior to the analysis, it can be difficult to identify the cause of that problem. Third, and most importantly, it is impossible to design an effective training program without first identifying the specific knowledge, skills, and abilities required to achieve goals or required to correct a problem. A needs analysis can be an essential part of the training development process because it helps to identify and inform about problems so possible solutions can be found.

There are a variety of steps that might be taken during a needs analysis, but most begin by collecting data related to the performance of each part of the organization. This information is usually gathered from surveys, interviews, observations, skill assessments, performance appraisals, etc. Once this information is collected, problems are identified within specific areas of the organization and solutions proposed. Advantages and disadvantages of each solution are then identified and the plan chosen that seems to provide the greatest benefit for the lowest cost.

Training

There are a variety of methods an organization can use to teach a particular skill, area of knowledge, or ability. However, some of the most common training methods used include case studies, demonstrations, group discussions, and lectures. A case study is a method in which the individual has the opportunity to apply certain skills, information, or abilities to a real-life situation. It allows the individual to learn how to perform a task or use a piece of information through practice. A demonstration is a method in which an instructor shows how to perform a particular task. A group discussion is a method in which a group learns a particular skill, ability, or piece of information by discussing that skill or the application of that skill. A lecture is a method in which an instructor tells how to perform a particular task.

There are a variety of factors to consider before choosing a training instructor for a training program, but the most important are the ability to teach and knowledge of the subject. Ability to teach is the ability to convey knowledge of a particular subject to other individuals. An instructor not only needs to know a subject, but also needs to be able to teach information about that subject to other employees. An instructor's ability to teach can usually be measured by assessing the individual's ability to present and communicate information clearly, the individual's ability to involve trainees in instruction, and the ability to present information in a logical and effective manner. The instructor's knowledge of the subject refers to how much the instructor knows about the subject, the amount of experience with the subject, and the ability to demonstrate the subject.

Pilot programs

Although there are a variety of ways to implement a pilot program, most organizations begin by identifying a test group to act as a suitable representation of the organization as a whole. This test group should consist of individuals that need to learn how to perform the specific task or improve the specific ability the training program has been designed for and should include members of management so they can see how the training program works. Most organizations will then attempt to decide whether part of the program or the entire program should be tested. It is usually better to test the entire program, but the costs or problems associated with implementing the entire program for a small group may be preventative. Finally, the program can be implemented and the results evaluated.

Organization development

Organization development is primarily intended to improve the organization's ability to identify and solve problems as effectively as possible. It usually focuses on development of internal systems for decision-making, systems for program development, systems for promoting progress towards organizational goals, systems for identifying problems, systems for handling problems that have been identified, etc. As a result, organization development refers to an approach that does not necessarily target one specific area of the organization, but instead refers to an approach that attempts to improve every part of the organization by constantly modifying the way the organization operates.

Organizational culture

Organizational culture refers to the system of beliefs and values that has been established in a particular organization and the way that individuals within the organization act based upon those values. In other words, organizational culture refers to the work environment that the employees and managers of the organization have created and continue to create as time passes. Most organizations attempt to modify or control the culture within the organization to some degree in order to make sure that the employees of the organization remain motivated. However, the culture of a particular organization is usually heavily influenced by the specific experiences of the members of the organization and by the outside environment surrounding the organization. As a result, it can sometimes be difficult for an organization to control its own culture especially when prominent figures in the organization become unhappy or outside influences begin placing a great deal of stress on the organization's employees.

Change management and organization development

Change management and organization development are two systems that are very closely related. In fact, organization development, in many ways, is actually a type of change management. This is because organization development refers to a series of processes and methods that can be used to modify the way that a particular aspect of the organization functions so the organization as a whole will function more effectively. Change management refers to a series of processes and methods that an organization can use to modify the way that a particular aspect of the organization functions with as little harm to the organization as possible. Both systems are related to implementing changes within the organization and, in many cases, organization development strategies may be used to help with the change management process and change management strategies may be used to minimize the risk of a negative impact associated with implementing the changes.

Kurt Lewin's change process theory

The two primary sources of change identified by Kurt Lewin's change process theory are the environment and the individual's needs. According to Kurt Lewin's change process theory, individuals change the way they function due to the environment and specific needs. Changes that occur due to environment include external factors, such as a request to perform the task more quickly.

According to Kurt Lewin's change process theory, the three stages of change are unfreezing, moving, and refreezing. Unfreezing is the attempt to remove barriers by making it clear that the change is necessary and must happen immediately. Moving is the attempt to implement the change and ensure each individual makes the change. Refreezing is the final stage of the change process in which the change becomes a normal part of the organization's functions and a determination about whether the change has produced the desired result. If the change has not produced the desired result, the process begins again and new changes are introduced.

Implementation theory

Implementation theory is the study and application of the specific methods and strategies used during the change process to bring about desired modifications within the organization. It refers to the process of identifying specific processes that can be used to implement changes and then implements those changes to benefit the organization overall. Implementation theory identifies the specific tools necessary to bring about change to begin the unfreezing, moving, and refreezing stages of the change process within the organization.

Organization development intervention

An organization development intervention is a specific strategy describing the plan an organization intends to use to bring about a particular change. If an organization has identified a particular problem or area that needs improvement, the specific strategy used to fix that problem or improve that area is known as an organization development intervention. These interventions include any action that can be used to influence a specific part of an organization. The three most common types of interventions are human process interventions, sociotechnical interventions, and techno-structural interventions.

A human process intervention is an organization development strategy to improve overall performance by changing the way members interact. Examples include the use of incentive

- 51 -

programs, the use of diversity programs, and the use of teambuilding activities. Incentive programs that encourage individuals with the appropriate knowledge and skills to enter the organization, encourage individuals to stay with the organization, and/or encourage individuals to perform up to or exceed the expectations of the organization can all help address problems. Diversity programs that place employees with different teams make it easier for each member of the organization to work together. Finally, teambuilding activities that encourage individuals to communicate and function effectively in groups can also help each individual move the organization towards a particular goal.

A sociotechnical intervention seeks to improve overall performance by changing the way that a particular group functions within the organization. Most sociotechnical interventions are specifically related to changes designed to make a particular group more self-sufficient. Specific examples of sociotechnical interventions include job enrichment, job rotation, and process improvement. Job enrichment is the practice of meeting new needs or un-addressed needs in the organization by increasing authority and responsibilities. Job rotation refers to the practice of periodically changing the specific tasks within the organization to ensure that each individual or group is capable of performing a variety of tasks. Process improvement refers to analyzing and changing the way a group performs a particular task.

A techno-structural intervention is an organization development strategy to improve overall performance by changing the way that work is performed within the organization. They are usually related to changes within the organization designed to ensure a specific process or piece of technology is used efficiently. One of the best examples of a techno-structural intervention is total quality management. Total quality management is a strategy to maintain the highest level of quality possible for the output produced by each specific task carried out by the organization. In most organizations, total quality management is implemented by using a series of procedures that are designed to establish a quality-oriented organizational culture and a system for monitoring and controlling the quality of each task performed.

Quality management

William Edwards Deming
William Edwards Deming was one of the first individuals to discuss quality management in detail and introduced a variety of concepts to the field of quality management. Two of his concepts form the basis for many of the quality management strategies used today. The first of these concepts is that the quality of a product or service can only be decided by the consumer. Even if an organization thinks a product or service is of high quality, it will not sell if the customer believes otherwise. Quality assessment must be based on the characteristics a consumer value. The second concept introduced by Deming was his 14-point system, which established a series of guidelines for quality management and the idea that an organization's top management is ultimately responsible for quality control.

Joseph Moses Juran
Joseph Moses Juran expanded on the concepts of William Edwards Deming and introduced a number of his own to the field of quality management. The first of these concepts was the idea that quality is determined by the consumer, but the needs of the organization have to be considered as well. Juran agreed with Deming that an organization had to assess the needs of the consumer to determine the quality of a product, but he made it clear that an organization must form processes and practices that would meet those needs. The second concept was the Juran Trilogy which established three stages an organization should go through during the quality management

process: quality planning, quality control, and quality improvement. Finally, Juran introduced the idea that the Pareto Principle could be applied to quality control and therefore 80% of the quality problems within an organization are related to 20% of the possible causes.

Juran Trilogy

The Juran Trilogy identifies three stages an organization must go through during the quality management process to ensure the organization can achieve the highest level of quality possible. The first stage is quality planning, in which the organization should identify the consumer's needs and work to implement practices and processes to meet those needs. The second stage is quality control in which the organization should monitor the quality achieved by each practice or process and ensure the result meets the needs of the organization and consumer. The third stage is quality improvement, which happens throughout the process and is the stage in which the organization attempts to solve quality problems or make specific processes more efficient by changing the way they are used.

Pareto analysis system

The Pareto analysis system, which was originally designed by Vilfredo Pareto, is a decision-making model that assumes that approximately 80% of the benefits an organization receives from a particular task are a result of 20% of the effort the individuals within the organization put into that task. However, in a quality control context, a Pareto analysis usually uses a second assumption made by the Pareto system, which is that 80% of the problems within the organization are typically caused by approximately 20% of the potential causes. In most cases, the Pareto analysis system is applied to quality control using a Pareto chart. A Pareto chart is a type of bar chart displaying each factor related to a particular problem, how frequently each of those factors actually causes the problem, and then arranges each factor from most frequent to least frequent. This is important because an organization, by identifying and charting the potential causes of a quality control issue, can identify the most influential factors and focus their quality control efforts on those factors.

Philip B. Crosby

Philip B. Crosby introduced a number of concepts to the field of quality management and attempted to change the way quality control is handled. One of the most important concepts introduced by Crosby, however, was his "Zero Defects" philosophy, which established the idea that the goal of any quality management program should be a product or service with no defects rather than an acceptable level of quality. This philosophy is part of "Philip Crosby's 14 Step Quality Improvement Process". Another important concept introduced by Crosby was his "doing it right the first time" (DIRFT) principle, which established four basic principles for quality management including quality: conformance to requirements, defect prevention is the best way to approach quality control, the goal of quality should be no defects, and quality can be measured by the price of nonconformance.

Philip B. Crosby's "doing it right the first time" (DIRFT) principle established four basic rules for how an organization should approach quality management. The first rule states that quality should be defined as conformance to requirements. An organization must identify and set specific requirements for each end product. The second rule of the principle states that defect prevention is the best way to approach quality control. It proposes the idea that an organization should find ways of preventing quality issues instead of using practices and procedures to fix problems repeatedly.

The third rule of the principle states that the goal of any organization should be "zero defects." An organization should implement processes and procedures to ensure all products meet the

- 53 -

requirements rather than accepting processes or practices that produce products that do not meet all of the desired requirements, but are considered "acceptable." The fourth rule of the principle states that quality can be measured by the price of nonconformance. Quality should be measured in terms of how much the organization will save by making sure a task is done right the first time instead of performing the task multiple times.

Dr. Kaoru Ishikawa

Dr. Kaoru Ishikawa introduced a variety of concepts to the field of quality management. One of the most important concepts states that the process does not end with production but should continue after the purchase is made to ensure customer satisfaction. If the customer is unhappy with a product, it is the responsibility of the organization to identify the problem and fix it. Ishikawa also helped to introduce the widespread use of charts, diagrams, and similar tools in quality assessment. In fact, he designed a cause and effect diagram for assessing quality.

A cause and effect diagram is designed to represent the factors causing a particular problem or the factors related to achieving a particular goal. It is usually used so each factor can be viewed and analyzed. A cause and effect diagram, which is also known as a fishbone or Ishikawa diagram, consists of a centerline with a series of lines branching off to form a tree or fishbone-like figure. The problem or goal is identified on the centerline of the figure and the categories that may lead to the desired goal or be related to the problem are identified at the end of each line branching off. Smaller lines then branch off each category line identifying specific factors that may have a negative or positive impact on the goal or problem.

There are a variety of charts and diagrams used to analyze problems within the organization. However, two of the most common are histograms and stratification charts. A histogram is a bar chart displaying each factor related to a problem and the number of times the problem occurs due to a particular factor. Histograms help prioritize which cause to address when a problem has been identified with a number of different causes. A stratification chart is a bar chart similar to a histogram except that it breaks each cause into more specific causes that may be related to the problem. Each specific cause and the number of occurrences for each cause category are represented with bars.

Six Sigma

Six Sigma is an approach to quality control, created by Motorola, Inc., designed to ensure products meet desired specifications through the use of a series of step-by-step quality control and product design processes. It is a strategy to reduce the number of defects by improving the system used to identify and eliminate problems related to quality. DMAIC (a Six Sigma approach) is a five-stage process designed to identify flaws by establishing a specific method for defining, measuring, analyzing, improving, and controlling quality.

DMAIC (Define, Measure, Analyze, Improve, and Control) is a five-stage process. In the first stage, end product requirements and the process for meeting those requirements are defined. In the second stage, the effectiveness of the process is measured by gathering information about the type and number of defects found. Then the information is analyzed and possible solutions are identified and implemented. The process is controlled by ensuring ongoing compliance.

Learning organizations

A learning organization is a company in which employees are encouraged to develop their knowledge, skills, and abilities so the organization will remain competitive and profitable as the business environment changes. This happens through initiatives promoting the open exchange of ideas, initiatives that reward individuals for exceptional performance, and initiatives that reward or allow employees to try out new ideas and apply those ideas to solve problems or improve the way certain tasks are performed.

According to Peter Senge, the five disciplines essential to a learning organization are mental models, personal mastery, shared vision, systems thinking, and team learning. A mental model is the need to understand the assumptions and beliefs affecting perception and acts based on those perceptions. Personal mastery is the need to have an area of expertise and the ability to increase their knowledge in that area. Shared vision is the need for a culture that encourages employees to work towards a common goal. Systems thinking is the ability to identify patterns and predict how those patterns might change in the future. Team learning refers to the idea that a team must be able to openly exchange ideas and put in as much effort as possible to achieve its goals.

Knowledge management

Knowledge management is a system of initiatives, practices, procedures, and processes used to ensure each member knows or can access all information necessary to perform responsibilities. Knowledge management can be important when there are a many employees working in different departments at different times. It is designed to ensure everyone has the same basic training and access to information from other departments to avoid performing the same task multiple times.

Andragogy and pedagogy

Andragogy and pedagogy are both sciences of how individuals learn. Andragogy is the study of how adults learn and focuses on making it easier to teach adults. Pedagogy, on the other hand, is the study of how children learn and focuses on making it easier to teach children. They are different fields because studies have found that children and adults learn in different ways. An instructor who understands these differences is able to identify the most effective teaching methods.

Malcolm Knowles' assumptions of learners

According to Malcolm Knowles, there are five assumptions typically made about adult learners. The first assumption, (motivation) is that they are internally motivated to learn by understanding why they need to learn. The second assumption (self-concept) is that they want to direct their own learning. The third assumption (adult experience) is that they want to apply what they already know as they learn and use their experience to help others learn. The fourth assumption (readiness) is that they are willing to learn if what they learn will help them in some way. The fifth assumption (orientation) is that they learn so they can apply knowledge to current rather than future problems.

According to Malcolm Knowles, there are five assumptions that can typically be made about child learners. The first assumption (motivation) is that they are externally motivated to learn due to other's expectations. The second assumption (self-concept) is that they want teachers, parents, etc. to guide their learning. The third assumption (child's experience) is that they learn more effectively by being taught because they do not have enough knowledge yet to apply it. The fourth assumption (readiness) is that they are willing to learn because society tells them to learn. The fifth assumption (orientation) is that they learn to be able to apply the information in the future.

Learning style

A learning style refers to the way an individual learns most effectively. Because each person learns information differently, some teaching methods are more effective than others. The three main learning styles are auditory, tactile, and visual and most. Training programs need to be designed to take different learning styles into consideration so participants will learn the material as efficiently as possible.

An auditory learner learns more effectively by hearing information rather than seeing it or using it. They usually learn most effectively by hearing descriptions or instructions such as lectures, group discussions, demonstrations of a particular sound (such as an alarm that might indicate a problem with a piece of machinery), or by listening to themselves read aloud.

A tactile learner learns more effectively by touching or using something rather than hearing it or seeing it. They usually learn most effectively by actually using a new tool or process, by actually being able to touch or move an object, or by physically applying the information in a controlled situation. They will have difficulty learning through verbal instructions (lectures or explanations) and visual methods (reading a handout). Learning activities include practicing techniques, role-playing, simulations, and other activities that allow the individual to learn through a "hands-on" approach.

A visual learner learns more effectively by seeing information rather than hearing or using it. They learn most effectively by seeing the information on a flashcard, chalkboard, handout or book, seeing a representation in a picture or diagram, watching videos or presentations, or by taking detailed notes and then rereading those notes. They have difficulty learning through verbal instruction (lectures and explanations) or by performing a task without written instructions or handouts.

Learning curve

A learning curve is a representation of the rate an individual learns. It is referred to as a curve because the rate changes over time. Learning curves are useful tools for instructors, human resource professionals, managers, and other individuals training or evaluating training programs by identifying learning patterns. Sudden changes in the learning curve may indicate a new training program is working effectively or that a change in the work environment is slowing the learning process.

Although there are a variety of learning curves encountered in an organization, there are some typical patterns. Some of these include negatively accelerating learning curves, plateau learning curves, positively accelerating learning curves, and S-shaped learning curves. A negatively accelerating curve is a curve that starts out increasing quickly, but begins to increase more slowly over time. A plateau learning curve starts out increasing quickly, but then stops. A positively accelerating learning curve starts out increasing slowly, but begins to increase rapidly over time. An S-shaped learning curve starts out increasing slowly, but over time increases more quickly, and then slows down again so the curve has an "S" shape.

Environmental factors of training

There are a variety of environmental factors that play a role in how effective a training program will be, but some of the most important factors relate to the training facility. Most people will have difficulty remaining focused if the location has poor ventilation, is too loud or distracting, does not

- 56 -

have enough seating or the seating is arranged so they cannot see or hear what is going on, or if the temperature in the location is too hot or too cold.

Seating styles

Banquet-style seating is an arrangement of round tables carefully distributed throughout meeting room. Each seat is positioned around the tables so each individual can see the others or turn to see a trainer or lecturer. Banquet-style seating is usually used to encourage teamwork or group discussion. Chevron-style seating is an arrangement in which desks, small tables, or chairs are arranged in small lines at either side of the room. Each line is angled so the people in the line can easily discuss information with the people beside, in front or behind them while still being able to see the trainer or lecturer. Chevron-style seating is usually used in narrow rooms, for large groups, or for programs or meetings with lecture and discussion.

Boardroom-style seating, also known as conference-style seating, is an arrangement in which a large table is placed in the center of the meeting room. Each seat is positioned around the table so that each person sees everyone else at the table. Boardroom-style seating is usually used for large discussions, meetings, or management training programs. U-shaped-style seating is an arrangement in which three long, narrow tables are placed at three sides of the room with at least one side of each table touching one side of another table to form a "U". Each seat is positioned around one of these three long tables so each person has a clear view of everything going on in the center of the room, the instructor, and everyone at the table. U-shaped-style seating is usually used for programs with a combination of presentations, lectures, discussions, etc.

Classroom-style seating is an arrangement in which long, narrow tables or lines of desks are arranged across the meeting room. Each seat is positioned around one of the tables or desks are positioned in lines so people can see the instructor and have a surface to take notes or fill-in handouts. Classroom-style seating is usually used for large groups and for presentations or lectures. Theatre-style seating is an arrangement in which chairs are arranged in lines across the room. Each chair is positioned so each person can see what is going on at the other side of the room. Theatre-style seating is usually used for large demonstrations, lectures, films, and presentations involving large groups.

Career development

The six stages of career development are assessment, investigation, preparation, commitment, retention, and transition. Assessment is the first stage where the person assesses strengths and weaknesses. Investigation is the second stage of the process where the person investigates the world to find careers to pursue. Preparation is the third stage where the person prepares by setting goals and learning new information, skills, and abilities. Commitment is the fourth stage and is where the person finds a job and commits to a career. Retention is the fifth stage of the process and is where the person maintains a career through additional networking and training. Transition is the final stage and is where the person transitions from one career to another.

There are a variety of methods to further a person's career development. Commonly used methods include coaching programs, employee counseling and support programs, and training workshops. Coaching programs are designed to provide each employee with a specialist to help learn new skills or understand how to handle work-related problems or situations. Employee counseling and support programs are designed to provide help if the employee is experiencing problems that may be affecting performance or the ability to seek other opportunities. Training workshops that offer employees the opportunity to learn the knowledge and skills associated with other positions within the organization can also be helpful.

There are a variety of methods a manager or supervisor can use to further an individual's career development. Some methods commonly used are coaching, counseling, mentoring, and evaluating. Employees can be coached to perform new tasks, handle certain problems outside of the scope of their current position, and develop communication and leadership. Employees can also be offered counseling, advice or emotional support. Managers or supervisors can act as mentors by helping employees apply for promotions, suggesting them for promotions, and offering guidance about other positions. Finally, managers or supervisors can help further an employee's career by evaluating their strengths and weaknesses.

There are a variety of methods individuals can use for their own career development. Some of the most important methods include attending training workshops, networking, and seeking additional education. Many organizations offer training workshops to help individuals seek management positions or positions in other departments, but most of these workshops are optional so they will only help if an individual actually takes the time to attend the program and learn the material. Networking is an essential part because it is nearly impossible to progress in an organization if there is unwillingness or an inability to establish relationships with managers, supervisors, co-workers, or customers. Finally, when the knowledge or educational background required for a particular position is lacking, the best way to develop a career is to seek additional education from colleges, universities, or seminars.

Management and leadership development

Management development is ensuring individuals have all the knowledge, skills, and abilities necessary to manage effectively. Leadership development is ensuring individuals have all the knowledge, skills, and abilities necessary to lead effectively. Management development is designed to teach an individual how to ensure each function is carried out as expected while leadership development is designed to teach an individual how to predict change within the business environment, identify the way the organization needs to change to meet those needs, and encourage other individuals to meet the changing needs of the organization.

Performance management

Performance management is any activity related to evaluating and improving the performance of each individual, team, and department. Performance management plays an essential role in human resource development, as it is impossible for an organization to function effectively if the tasks necessary for the organization's operations are not consistently carried out as expected. Human resource development is designed to provide the organization with individuals that have the skills and knowledge necessary for the organization to achieve its goals and performance management is designed to evaluate whether the members of the organization are helping the organization achieve those goals or not. As a result, even though performance management and human resource development are two separate processes, they both work together to identify and eliminate performance problems so the organization can continue to function normally and ultimately continue to make progress towards it goals.

The performance management process can vary from organization to organization, but most organizations use a process that consists of three basic steps. The first step of the process that most organizations use consists of establishing the goals that the organization wants to achieve, identifying the tasks and skills required to achieve those goals, and informing employees of the appropriate way to carry out tasks and responsibilities in order to achieve these goals. This step is usually carried out by the organization's executives, decision-makers, and HR professionals through goal setting, needs analysis, the creation of corporate value statements and a code of conduct, and other similar processes. Once the organization has set goals and informed employees of the appropriate way to carry out each task, the organization's supervisors and managers need to monitor the tasks performed by each employee, identify and document performance problems, and inform employees of the problems and the appropriate way to fix these problems. Finally, at the end of each year or other set period, the organization needs to conduct in-depth appraisals of the performance of each employee.

Performance appraisal

It is important for an organization to train performance evaluators to use appropriate appraisal methods because a performance appraisal is only useful to the organization if it is fair and accurate. This is because an organization's performance management process relies heavily on the ability of the organization to identify and eliminate performance problems. As a result, a performance appraisal must offer an accurate view of an individual's performance so the organization can accurately identify problem areas or performance issues and then improve these problem areas or handle these issues appropriately. However, there are a number of different factors, such as the evaluator's own biases or the appraisal process that the evaluator uses, which can influence a performance appraisal so it can often be extremely difficult for a manager or supervisor to conduct an appraisal that is completely fair and accurate. Therefore, in order to make sure that each manager or supervisor conducts each appraisal as effectively as possible the organization must train each manager or supervisor to use the appropriate set of appraisal methods.

The four main types of performance appraisals are behavioral appraisal methods, comparison appraisal methods, essay/narrative appraisal methods, and rating appraisal methods. Behavioral appraisal methods identify the most important tasks related to each position, the specific way the employee is expected to behave to perform that task, and establishes a system of descriptions describing how effectively the individual behaved. Comparison appraisal methods compare the performance of an employee with other employees. Essay/narrative appraisal methods are used by a manager or supervisor to describe an employee's performance in writing. Rating appraisal methods use a checklist or scale to rate the individual's performance.

There are a several behavioral appraisal methods, but the most common is a method known as BARS. BARS (Behaviorally Anchored Rating Scales) analyzes the job description for a particular position and identifies the tasks that must be performed for the organization to function effectively. Once the tasks are identified, a determination is made about the specific way the individual should behave to perform each task. For example, if communication is identified as a necessary skill for a management position, an individual in that position must be able to keep others "in the loop." A series of statements that are ranked is then designed describing how effectively the individual behaved. Performance evaluators can then choose the statement that best describes the employee's behavior.

There are several comparison appraisal methods, but the three most common are the forced distribution method, the paired-comparison method, and the ranking method. The forced-distribution method, also known as forced ranking, uses a bell curve in which the majority of employees will receive an average score and a small group will receive extremely high or extremely low performance scores. The paired-comparison method compares the performance of each member of a specific group with another group. The ranking method ranks each employee based on performance from the most to least effective.

There are a variety of essay/narrative appraisal methods, but the three most common are the critical incident method, the essay method, and the field review method. The critical incident method documents each performance problem related to an employee occurring during a set period so the evaluator can discuss problems with the employee at the end. The essay method is a method in which performance evaluators write a short essay for each employee describing the employee's performance during the performance period. The field review method is a method in which an individual other than the employee's direct supervisor or manager performs the appraisal and writes down a series of assessments and observations about that particular employee's performance.

There is a variety of rating appraisal methods, but the two most common are the checklist method and the rating scale method. The checklist method is a series of statements describing a certain level of performance. The performance evaluator can then check a box next to the statement that best describes the individual's performance in each performance area. The rating scale method rates an individual's performance on a point scale, usually a 1 - 3, 1 - 4, 1 - 5, or 1 - 10 scale with lower numbers representing poor performance and higher numbers representing superior performance.

Total Rewards

Total rewards

The concept known as total rewards refers to all of the compensation and benefits received for performing tasks related to each position. It is important to have an effective total rewards program for two main reasons. First, it encourages employees to join and then stay with the organization. Secondly, there are legal concerns associated with the minimum amount of compensation an individual can receive for a certain amount of work making it essential to consider these concerns to avoid unnecessary fines or litigation.

Types of rewards
The two main types of rewards used to compensate employees are monetary and non-monetary. Monetary compensation is any tangible reward provided as payment for work, including salary and wages, paid sick days, paid vacation time, retirement plans, and stock options. Non-monetary compensation is any intangible reward provided to encourage an individual to perform work, including better assignments, employee-of-the-month awards, flexible scheduling, and special privileges.

An organization can issue monetary compensation to employees through direct or indirect compensation. Direct compensation is any monetary compensation paid directly to the employee, including salary or wages, bonuses, overtime, or special pay. Indirect compensation is monetary compensation paid to a third party on the employee's behalf or paid without the employee having to perform work, including health insurance, paid sick days, paid vacation time, retirement plans, and stock options.

Philosophy
A total rewards philosophy is developed to clearly state reward goals and how those goals will be achieved. Identifying this philosophy is helpful to ensure the rewards are reflecting the values and goals of an organization or if they need to be modified.
The two types of total reward philosophies are entitlement philosophies and performance-based philosophies. An entitlement philosophy issues rewards based on the length of time a particular employee has been with the organization. It assumes an individual is entitled to certain rewards because of seniority or length of time in a specific position. Entitlement philosophies encourage individuals to stay with the organization, but do not necessarily encourage effective performance. A performance-based philosophy, on the other hand, issues rewards for good performance.

Strategy
A total rewards strategy is a plan used to design a total rewards program. It is based on the organization's total rewards philosophy and is primarily designed to establish the framework for the allocation of program resources. It refers to the various ways resources are used to encourage individuals to work for the organization without exceeding limits. Because of the limited number of resources, it is essential to find ways to attract and keep employees.

There are a variety of factors to consider when designing an effective total rewards strategy. The four main factors include the competitive environment, the economic environment, the labor market, and the legal environment. The competitive environment is the effect competition has on the ability to allocate resources to the total rewards program. For example, if competitors are offering a specific product at a price that is far lower, the organization may need to reduce the amount of funds allocated to its total rewards program to afford a price reduction. The economic environment refers to the effect the economy has on the cost of labor. For example, as the cost of living increases, the cost of labor will usually increase as well. The labor market is the availability of skilled employees and the legal environment refers to taxes and regulations.

Employees and independent contractors

It is important to determine whether an individual is an employee of the organization or an independent contractor for several reasons. First, an organization is required to pay half of an employee's social security tax and to withhold federal and state taxes from an employee's pay, but not for independent contractors. Secondly, an organization is required to pay overtime, on-call pay, and special pay to an employee under certain conditions, but not to an independent contractor. Finally, many of the legal protections granted to employees do not cover independent contractors.

According to the IRS, there are three groups of factors when considering whether an individual should be considered an employee or an independent contractor. These three groups of factors relate to the organization's behavioral control over the individual (or the ability to control how the individual conducts work), the organization's financial control over the individual (or the ability to control how much the individual will profit from the performance of work), and the type of relationship between the organization and the individual. The type of relationship refers to whether the individual is under contract or not and whether or not that contract forms a permanent arrangement that makes it difficult for the individual to perform work for other organizations.

According to the Department of Labor (DOL), there are seven factors an organization should consider when determining whether an individual should be considered an employee or an independent contractor. First, is the relationship with the individual temporary or permanent? Second, how important is the task and to what extent could the organization function without someone performing that task? Third, how much control is needed over the individual? Fourth, how much has the individual invested in the facilities and equipment used to perform the work? Fifth, is the individual required to make decisions related to competing in an open market or does the organization make these decisions? Sixth, does the individual operate independently of the organization? Finally, what is the individual's risk of profit/loss?

Davis Bacon Act

The Davis Bacon Act, which was passed in 1931, is designed to prevent employees working in the construction industry from receiving substandard wages. This act requires any employer in the construction industry with $2,000 or more in federal contracts or any employer in the construction industry with $2,000 or more in federal funding to pay each employee working at the construction site a wage equal to or greater than the prevailing wage for the area in which the construction site is located. The prevailing wage for a particular area is defined as the wage of an individual performing a similar local job. This act is important because it establishes a regulation related to the minimum amount an organization can pay an employee.

Walsh-Healy Public Contracts Act

The Walsh-Healy Public Contracts Act, which was passed in 1936, is designed to prevent employees working under government contract from receiving substandard wages. This act requires any employer with $10,000 or more in federal contracts to pay each employee a wage equal to or

- 62 -

greater than the prevailing wage for the area in which the work is performed. This is defined as the wage of an individual performing a similar local job. This act also required employers to pay overtime pay equal to 1 and ½ times an individual's regular wage for each hour in excess of 8 hours in a day or for each hour in excess of 40 hours in a week. In addition to establishing wage regulations, this act also prevents employers from hiring children under the age of 18 or hiring individuals convicted of a crime, and requires the workplace to meet safety and sanitation standards.

FLSA

The Fair Labor Standards Act (FLSA), which was passed in 1938, is designed to prevent employees from receiving substandard wages and to prevent organizations from employing children except in very specific situations. It established regulations related to the minimum wage, situations an employer is required to pay overtime or on-call pay, keeping payroll records, and minimum age to perform certain types of work and length of work time. This act usually applies to employers with at least two employees that have $500,000 or more in annual sales or any employer that engages in interstate commerce of any kind. It does not apply to employers covered by another labor standard law specific to their industry.

Minimum wage

The Fair Labor Standards Act (FLSA) established regulations designed to prevent employees from receiving substandard wages and established the minimum wage. The federal minimum wage is the smallest amount an employer can pay for each hour of work and they are required to pay at least the amount specified by the federal minimum wage to any nonexempt employee. An employee will be considered exempt from this provision if the individual receives a weekly salary of at least $455, if the employee works in a profession not covered by the FLSA or a profession identified as exempt from the minimum wage provision of the FLSA, or if the employer has received special permission to pay less than the minimum wage as part of a Department of Labor program.

There are two situations in which an organization may need to pay an employee more than the federal minimum wage. First, if the individual has worked more than 40 hours in a single week and is in a position covered by the Fair Labor Standards Act, he/she is entitled to overtime pay for each additional hour over 40 hours. Secondly, when the minimum wage for the state in which the organization's employees are located is higher than the federal minimum wage. However, most states have their own list of exemptions and requirements so that a particular organization may be part of an industry covered by the Fair Labor Standards Act, but not by the regulations set by state law.

Overtime

The Fair Labor Standards Act established regulations designed to prevent employees from receiving substandard wages, especially related to overtime pay. It defines overtime pay as 1 and ½ times the regular wage normally received and establishes that overtime pay must be paid to any nonexempt individual working more than 40 hours in a single week. The number of hours an individual has worked in a given week does not include hours paid for vacation time, sick leave, paid holidays, or similar pay received when work is not actually performed. Certain states may have overtime regulations in addition to those established by the Fair Labor Standards Act.

On-call

The Fair Labor Standards Act established regulations designed to prevent employees from receiving substandard wages especially related to on-call pay. This regulation requires an employer to pay regular wages if the employee is required to wait at the job site ready to perform work as it becomes available. This must be paid to the employee even if the individual is not actually performing work as he or she waits. However, this regulation does not apply to individuals on-call at any location other than the job site.

<u>Record keeping</u>
The Fair Labor Standards Act established regulations requiring employers to record information related to an employee's personal information, pay period, and pay. Personal information required to be recorded are name, address, occupation, and the individual's date of birth if 18 or younger. Pay period information includes the specific day and time the pay period begins, the date payment is issued for the period, the total hours worked by the individual each day, and for the period. The specific pay includes the total regular pay an individual receives per day, the total overtime pay received for the period, the regular wage if overtime is worked, the total pay received for the period, any deductions such as tax withholdings from the individual's pay, and any additions such as bonuses.

<u>Child labor</u>
The Fair Labor Standards Act established child labor regulations designed to prevent children from entering the workforce before they are mature enough to do so, from working in hazardous environments, from working for long periods, and from working instead of attending school. These regulations prohibit employers from hiring anyone under the age of 14 unless the individual is working for a parent or for a farm and from hiring individuals under the age of 18 for any kind of work deemed hazardous by law. These regulations also prevent individuals under the age of 16 from working in any manufacturing or mining-related job, working during school hours, working more than 3 hours a day or 18 hours a week during a school week or 8 hours a day and 40 hours a week during a non-school week, and working before 7:00 a.m. or past 7:00 p.m. during the school year or working before 7:00 a.m. or past 9:00 p.m. during the summer.

Portal-to-Portal Act

The Portal-to-Portal Act, which was passed in 1947, is an amendment to the Fair Labor Standards Act designed to define the difference between compensable time and time that is not compensable. It sets specific criteria for the situations an employer needs to pay an employee and the situations an employer does not need to pay an employee. It requires an employer to pay an employee covered by the Fair Labor Standards Act for any time the employee is performing a task related to a particular position including travel time if that time is not part of the individual's regular commute and any time spent waiting to begin work by request of the employer. The employer is not required to pay the employee for regular commuting time or any other period the individual is not performing a task required by the position or specifically requested by the employer.

Equal Pay Act

The Equal Pay Act, which was passed in 1963, prevents wage discrimination based on gender. It requires an employer to provide equal pay to both men and women performing similar tasks unless the employer can prove that there is an acceptable reason for the difference in pay, such as merit, seniority, quantity or quality of work performed, etc. This act also establishes the criteria that must be considered to determine whether a particular position is similar or not. This includes the effort necessary for the tasks related to the position, the level of responsibility associated with the position, the skills required to perform the position, and the working conditions associated with the position.

Job evaluations

It is important to conduct a job evaluation during the total rewards planning process for two major reasons. First, a job evaluation identifies the positions most important to success so rewards can be assigned appropriately. Secondly, to determine whether there should be a difference in pay between two positions. For example, a secretary and an administrative assistant with the same skills and performing similar jobs should receive equal pay even though they have different titles.

A compensable factor is a specific characteristic of a position used to determine the value of that position. They are specific job requirements considered important and individuals are compensated based on their ability to meet these requirements. Compensable factors are commonly used during a job evaluation to compare the requirements of a variety of different positions. Some of the most common compensable factors relate to knowledge, skills, and abilities. These factors include characteristics related to a particular position such as experience required, level of education required, level of responsibility required, and knowledge of specific technology or processes required.

The two main types of job evaluation techniques used to determine the value of a particular position are non-quantitative techniques and quantitative techniques. Non-quantitative techniques, also referred to as whole job methods, are techniques to evaluate the skills and abilities associated with a particular position and assigning a value based on whether it requires more or less skill than other jobs within the organization. Quantitative techniques, also referred to as nontraditional techniques or factor-based methods, are techniques of assigning a specific value to each factor in a series of compensable factors identified as important. The organization can then evaluate each position, determine how many compensable factors are required for the position, and can assign a value to the position by using a mathematical formula.

The three most common non-quantitative job evaluation techniques are the classification method, the pricing method, and the ranking method. The classification method separates positions into categories based on tasks. Each category is then listed in order of its importance and assigned pay based on the importance of its category. The pricing method, also known as the slotting method, assigns a value to a position equal to the value of a similar position or category that already exists. Finally, the ranking method ranks each position from lowest to highest based on how the skills and abilities required to perform the position compare with those associated with other positions.

The most common quantitative job evaluation techniques are the factor comparison method and the point factor method. The factor comparison method identifies a series of compensable factors and establishes a ranking system to measure how much of a particular compensable factor, such as education, is required for a particular position. Each factor ranking is assigned a specific dollar value and the value of the position is determined by adding the total dollar value for the rank of each factor required for the position. The point factor method is very similar, but it assigns a point value to each factor rank instead of a dollar value and the pay for the position is determined by comparing the total amount of points to a chart.

Base pay

Three of the most important factors involved in determining the appropriate base pay for a new employee are the value of the position, the education and experience of the individual, and the demand for individuals able to fill the position. The value of the position refers to the value identified during the job evaluation process based on the importance of the position to the organization. The education and experience refers to the knowledge, skills, and abilities the individual has beyond the minimum requirements necessary to perform the position. The demand for individuals able to fill the position refers to the ability of the individual to seek employment with another organization and the ease or difficulty the organization would have in replacing the employee.

Differential and variable pay

Both differential pay and variable pay refer are used to encourage individuals to perform work for an organization. However, differential pay is used specifically to encourage the performance of a task most people do not want to perform. Variable pay is used to persuade an employee to perform more effectively. The difference is that differential pay is given to an individual to ensure an essential task is performed while variable pay is awarded to an individual for achieving a specific organizational goal.

Some of the most common types of differential pay include hazard pay, on-call pay, and shift pay. Hazard pay is for performing dangerous or extremely unpleasant work such as handling chemicals, working in extremely harsh environments, or working in environments that risk exposure to disease, infection, or radiation. On-call pay is when the employee is required to report to work on extremely short notice. Shift pay is for working unusual hours such as an evening or overnight shifts.

Some of the most common variable pay programs include individual incentive programs, gainsharing programs, and profit sharing programs. An individual incentive program pays a specific amount or a percentage of base pay if the employee achieves a specific goal set by the organization. A gainsharing program encourages the achievement of certain financial goals by offering a percentage of the money the organization earns or saves from achieving that goal. A profit sharing program encourages the achievement of certain goals by offering a percentage of the profit when goals are met.

Salary surveys

A salary survey is an assessment of the compensation and benefits currently offered by organizations in a particular labor market. It is a collection of information related to how each organization encourages employees to work in the current economic environment. These surveys are usually conducted by individuals or third-parties outside the organization and are an essential part of a total rewards planning process because they identify changes in the current labor market that may impact effectiveness.

The three most common types of salary surveys are commissioned surveys, government surveys, and industry surveys. A commissioned survey is prepared from outside the organization. Because these surveys are expensive, they are used to obtain very specific information related to the labor market. A government survey is prepared by a government agency such as the Bureau of Labor Statistics and usually accomplished without cost to the organization. However the information is less specific than the information included in other types of surveys. An industry survey is prepared by the members of a particular industry. They are relatively inexpensive and provide more specific information than government surveys.

Pay structure

A pay structure is the compensation system an organization uses to determine the appropriate base pay for positions by separating each job into categories based on value to the organization. Pay structure is an essential part of any organization's total rewards program because it establishes a guide for appropriate hourly wages or salaries. Specific base pay minimums and maximums for each category are well-defined and avoid arbitrarily assigning pay.

Creating a pay structure can vary greatly, but most organizations begin the process by conducting a job evaluation for each position. Once each position is evaluated and assigned a value, they are categorized based on their value to the organization. The organization will usually gather information from salary surveys to determine the market median for each category, and wages an individual would receive at the midpoint of a similar pay category for another organization. Finally, a pay range is developed for each category.

Broadbanding

Broadbanding is a type of pay structure design in which an organization creates a very small number of broadly defined pay grades into which all jobs are separated, i.e. general staff, management, and executives. Organizations usually choose to use a broadbanding approach to encourage teamwork and eliminate problems arising from perceived differences in status between different pay grades. The focus is on performance rather than activities related to achieving promotions.

Wage compression

Wage compression is any situation where an employee is hired at a higher wage than employees receive who have similar skills and are already with the organization in a similar position. It is important to avoid wage compression because it leads to staffing and performance problems as current employees become dissatisfied and unmotivated because of the perceived arbitrary nature of pay decisions.

Compa-ratio

A compa-ratio is a mathematical formula used to compare a specific employee's pay with the pay at the middle of the pay range. A compa-ratio is expressed as a percentage and can be determined by dividing the employee's base salary by the midpoint salary for the employee's pay range (base salary / midpoint salary = compa-ratio.) For example, if an individual is in a pay grade that ranges from \$25,000 to 45,000 a year and the individual receives \$30,000 a year, the midpoint of the range is equal to (\$25,000 + 45,000) / 2 or \$35,000 and the compa-ratio is equal to \$30,000 / \$35,000, which is equal to 0.857 or 85.7%. Compa-ratios are primarily used to compare an employee's current pay with the pay of other employees in similar positions to determine whether the individual is receiving a fair amount considering seniority, performance, etc.

ERISA

The Employee Retirement Income Security Act (ERISA), which was passed in 1974, is designed to protect individuals from benefit plans operating with questionable methods. This act requires an employer or the benefit plan administrator working for an employer to provide information about benefits, system for obtaining benefits, and financial reports associated with a benefit plan to any employee participating in the plan. It also requires a benefit plan to allow any individual over the age of 21 that has performed at least 1,000 hours of work for the organization to participate in the plan. In addition to these regulations, it specifically holds benefit plan administrators responsible for designing and operating plans in the best interest of the plan's participants. It is important to note this act does not require an organization to establish a benefit plan, but instead requires any private organization choosing to establish a benefit plan to follow these regulations.

OWBPA

The Older Worker Benefit Protection Act (OWBPA), which was passed in 1990, is an amendment to the Age Discrimination in Employment Act designed to prevent employers from unfairly refusing benefits to individuals over a certain age. This act prohibits an employer or benefit plan administrator from preventing participation or continuing to participate in a benefits program due to age if the individual is covered by the Age Discrimination in Employment Act. It establishes that an employer may only set a maximum age limit or reduce an individual's benefits due to age in situations in which the age limit or age-related reduction can be shown to significantly reduce the costs associated with implementing the benefit plan. The act also specifically establishes that an employer may implement a plan or system based on seniority as long as the plan does not require an individual to leave the program after a certain age.

REA

The Retirement Equity Act (REA), which was passed in 1984, is an amendment to the Employee Retirement Income Security Act (ERISA) designed to establish a number of benefit plan regulations in addition to those originally established by ERISA. These regulations are designed to protect spouses from losing their benefits after a plan participant's death or after a divorce, but also include regulations to strengthen the protections offered by ERISA. Protections established by REA include regulations prohibiting benefit plan administrators from considering maternity/paternity leave as a break in service regarding the right to participate in a plan or become vested in a plan, regulations that require pension plans to automatically provide benefits to a spouse in the event of the plan participant's death unless a waiver has been signed by both the spouse and the participant, and regulations that lowered the age an employer had to allow an individual to participate in a pension plan.

Pension Protection Act

The Pension Protection Act, which was passed in 2006, is an amendment to the Employee Retirement Income Security Act (ERISA) designed to protect individuals from pension plans that do not have enough funding to pay out all of the retirement benefits promised to employees. This act requires any employer establishing a pension plan to make contributions in amounts large enough to ensure the plan is not under funded and requires employers to offer at least three investment options in addition to the employer's own stock if the employer's stock is offered as part of a benefit plan. This act also allows employers to include employees in an organization's 401(k) program with or without the permission of the individual as long as the individual has the right to opt-out of the plan.

COBRA

The Consolidated Omnibus Budget Reconciliation Act (COBRA), which was passed in 1985, is an amendment to the Employee Retirement Income Security Act (ERISA) designed to ensure employees leaving an organization or employees having their hours reduced below the minimum necessary to participate in a group health insurance plan still have access to the health insurance offered by the employer. This act requires any employer with at least 20 employees to offer an employee the opportunity to continue coverage if the individual terminated employment, the individual's hours were reduced below the participation limit, of if the employer terminated employment unless terminated for gross misconduct. This act also requires any employer with at least 20 employees to offer an employee's spouse or dependents access to the health insurance offered by the employer if specific qualifying events occur. If an employee, spouse, or dependent chooses to continue coverage, the employer may require the individual to pay the full insurance premium.

The Consolidated Omnibus Budget Reconciliation Act (COBRA) is designed to ensure employees and their families still have access to the health insurance plan offered by an employee's former employer. For an employee's spouse or dependent to be covered under COBRA, a specific qualifying event must occur. An employee's spouse or dependent will be covered under COBRA if the employee terminates employment, the employee's hours are reduced below the participation limit, the employer terminated employment unless for gross misconduct, the employee and the spouse become legally separated or divorce and the employee is eligible for COBRA coverage, the employee becomes eligible for Medicare and is eligible for COBRA coverage, or if the employee dies and was eligible for COBRA coverage. An employee's dependents will also be eligible for COBRA coverage if the dependents lose dependent child status according to the rules established by the insurance plan.

The Consolidated Omnibus Budget Reconciliation Act (COBRA) is designed to ensure employees and their families still have access to the health insurance plan offered by an employee's former employer. However, COBRA coverage only lasts for a set amount of time after a qualifying event occurs. If an employee, spouse, or dependent claims coverage because the employee has terminated employment, the employee's hours have been reduced below the participation limit, the employer terminated employment unless for gross misconduct, or the dependent lost dependent child status, the individual may receive insurance coverage from the employer for up to18 months. If an employee's spouse or dependent claims coverage because the employee is eligible for Medicare and is eligible for COBRA coverage, the individual may receive coverage for up to 29 months. If an employee's spouse or dependent claims coverage for a divorce or the death of the employee, the individual may receive coverage for up to 36 months.

HIPAA

The Health Insurance Portability and Accountability Act (HIPAA), which was passed in 1996, is an amendment to the Employee Retirement Income Security Act (ERISA). In addition to addressing certain privacy concerns, it is designed to ensure employees and their families have access to health insurance coverage even if they have a preexisting medical condition. This act prohibits an employer from refusing to cover an individual under the employer's health insurance plan or charging the individual a higher rate for the plan because of a preexisting medical condition. This act allows the employer or the employer's health care provider to refuse coverage of any costs directly related to the preexisting condition for a period of 12 months for individuals enrolled during a normal enrollment period or 18 months for individuals that enrolled during a late enrollment period if the individual was not previously covered by another health insurance plan.

In addition to ensuring employees have access to health insurance coverage, HIPAA protects the privacy of health information that could be linked to a specific individual. Health information that could be used to identify a particular individual must be safeguarded because the Department of

Health and Human Services (HHS) has identified it as protected health information (PHI.) These activities include creating a written plan for protecting the privacy of PHI, implementing procedures to protect and prevent the misuse of PHI, training employees regarding the privacy requirements set by the HIPAA act, and other activities related to protecting an individual's personal health information.

MHPA

The Mental Health Parity Act (MHPA), which was passed in 1996, is designed to prevent health plan providers from setting limits on mental health benefits that are stricter than the limits the provider has set for other health benefits. This act prohibits a health plan provider from setting a financial cap on the amount the health plan provider will pay for mental health benefits if that cap is lower than the cap the provider has set for other benefits. This act applies to any health plan provider providing coverage for an employer with at least 51 employees, but only if the regulations set by this act will not result in a 1% or greater increase in the costs of the provider. It is also important to note that health plan providers are not required to offer mental health benefits and providers may set other limits related to mental health coverage as long as there is no specific payout limit.

FMLA

The Family Medical Leave Act (FMLA), which was passed in 1993, protects employees needing a temporary leave of absence from losing their employment or benefits as a result. This act requires an employer to allow each employee up to 12 weeks of unpaid leave during a 12-month period if the individual is unable to work due to a serious health condition, needs to care for an immediate family member with a serious health condition, or needs to care for his or her newly born or newly adopted child. This act also requires an employer to allow the individual to retain current health coverage if the individual is receiving coverage from the employer. Once, the leave period has ended, the employer is required to allow the original position to be taken back.

FMLA applies to any employer with at least 50 employees and applies to any public or educational agency. However, to be covered by this act, the employer must employ at least 50 employees working within 75-miles of the worksite, unless the individual is employed by a public agency or an educational agency. The employee taking the leave must also have worked at least 1,250 hours during the 12 months prior to the leave and must have worked for the employer for a period of at least 12 months.

The Family Medical Leave Act only protects an individual taking his or her leave to care for a newly born or newly adopted child, caring for a family member with a serious health condition, or cannot work because of suffering from a serious health condition. According to the Family Medical Leave Act, a serious health condition is "an illness, injury, impairment, or physical or mental condition" that incapacitates an individual. A condition that incapacitates an individual refers to any condition in which an individual must receive treatment while staying at an inpatient care facility such as a hospital or any condition preventing the individual from working and performing other daily tasks for at least three days for which an individual must receive continuing treatment.

OASDI

The Old Age, Survivors, and Disability Insurance (OASDI) program, which was established by the Social Security Act (SSA) of 1935, offers benefits to employees that have retired or become disabled. This program requires employees to pay a percentage of their income to the federal government and requires employers to match the contributions made by their employees. As employees contribute to the fund, they will receive social security credits and may receive up to four social security credits a year based on the amount paid into the fund. If an individual becomes completely disabled for a period of at least five consecutive months or retires at age 62 or older, he/she is entitled to receive a portion of previous earnings from the social security program. To receive retirement benefits from social security, the individual must have at least 40 credits before retiring.

Federal-State Unemployment Insurance Program

The Federal-State Unemployment Insurance Program, which was established as part of the Social Security Act of 1935, offers benefits to employees who have lost their employment. This program requires employers to pay a state unemployment insurance (SUI) tax to help individuals seeking employment after losing a position. The tax rate an employer must pay and the requirements for an employee to be eligible for unemployment benefits vary from state to state. However, most states require an individual to work for a specific period of time prior to claiming unemployment and to actively seek employment while receiving benefits. If an individual is eligible for unemployment, a portion of his or her previous pay may be received for up to 26 weeks. It is important to note, however, that most states will not allow an individual to claim any unemployment benefits if the individual was terminated due to the individual's own actions.

Medicare

The Medicare program, which was established by an amendment made to the Social Security Act in 1965, offers health insurance coverage to elderly and/or disabled individuals. This program consists of four benefit areas referred to as parts and each part offers a specific type of coverage to the individual. Medicare Part A covers inpatient care including hospital stays and home nursing as long as that nursing care is not part of rehabilitation. Medicare Part B covers an individual's outpatient care including physicals, vaccinations, and tests. Medicare Part B also covers the costs associated with certain medical equipment, such as wheelchairs. Medicare Part C is an alternative to Medicare Part A in which an individual may choose to be covered by a private rather than the federal government plan. Finally, Medicare Part D offers a variety of prescription drug plans an individual may choose.

It is possible for an individual to be eligible for certain parts of the program and be ineligible for other parts. To be covered by Part A, the individual must be at least 65 years old and eligible to receive social security or railroad retirement benefits. An individual may also be eligible to receive benefits from Medicare Part A if the individual has been disabled for a period of at least 24 months or has a qualifying disability and is eligible to receive social security disability benefits. To be covered by Part B, the individual must be at least 65 years old or be eligible for Medicare Part A under the disability provision. To be covered by Part C or Part D, the individual must be eligible for Medicare part A and must be currently covered by Part B.

USERRA

The Uniformed Services Employment and Reemployment Rights Act (USERRA), which was passed in 1994, protects individuals serving in the military from losing their employment or being denied employment. It prohibits an employer from refusing to hire an individual who is a member of the military or is about to become a member of the military, from refusing to allow an individual to retake his or her previous position after a leave of absence to serve for the military, and from refusing to promote or offer certain benefits because of the individual's military status. This act also requires an employer to inform all employees of these regulations by posting the regulations in a location that can be viewed by all employees or by informing employees of these regulations in another way.

Benefits

Types
The two main types of benefits are voluntary and involuntary benefits. Voluntary benefits are benefits chosen to achieve a specific goal such as encouraging individuals to join the organization and/or stay with the organization. Voluntary benefits include 401(k) plans, dental insurance plans, health insurance plans, profit sharing plans, vacation pay, and other benefits an organization is not required to implement. Involuntary benefits are benefits an organization is required to implement by a local, state, or federal law. Involuntary benefits include social security, unemployment insurance, unpaid family leave, worker's compensation, and any other benefits an organization is legally required to implement.

The three main types of voluntary benefits are deferred benefits, health and welfare benefits, and work-life balance benefits. Deferred benefits are not received immediately, but at some future point (like retirement). Health and welfare benefits are those that help pay for medical costs or with any other costs associated with an unexpected emergency or event. Health and welfare benefits are usually provided in the form of insurance. Work-life balance benefits are those that allow an individual to perform the day-to-day activities that must performed outside of work to function normally. Work-life balance benefits allow an individual to "balance" work responsibilities with other responsibilities. Work-life benefits are usually related to time-off or flexible hours.

Plans
A defined-benefit plan is a retirement plan in which an organization promises an individual will receive a specific amount of money each month after retirement. The amount is usually determined using a formula that takes the individual's monthly pay and length of time with the company into consideration. A defined contribution plan is a retirement plan in which an organization contributes money into an account. The amount may be in addition to the individual's pay or taken out of the individual's pay. As money is placed into the account, the money is invested to offer a larger retirement benefit to the individual at the time he or she retires. However, since there is always some risk associated with any investment, the amount that a specific individual will receive upon retirement with a defined contribution plan can vary greatly.

A cash balance plan is a retirement plan in which an organization promises an employee will receive a set amount of money at retirement. Most organizations determine this amount by establishing the amount the account should increase each month and calculating the amount the account would have when the individual retires. The needed amount can then be determined to deposit into the employee's cash balance plan account annually, with interest taken into consideration, to ensure the account has the appropriate balance at retirement. A simplified employee pension plan is a retirement plan contributed to by both the organization and the employee into an individual retirement account (IRA.) Organizations contributing to an employee's IRA can either match the amount that the employee contributes to the account or establish a set contribution rate.

Medical programs
A health maintenance organization (HMO) program is health care insurance that is used to minimize the costs associated with expensive procedures and examinations by encouraging employees to take part in activities that diminish the need for them. Most HMO programs control

- 72 -

access to expensive procedures and examinations by requiring an employee to choose a primary care physician that must approve any special procedures or examinations. A preferred provider organization (PPO) program is health care insurance used to minimize medical costs by requiring an individual to seek care from a specific network of health care facilities and physicians. Most PPO's allow an individual to seek care from outside the network as well, but the individual will usually be responsible for a much larger portion of the costs related to the medical care.

<u>Insurance types</u>

Dental insurance is a health and welfare benefit in which a certain amount of the individual's dental costs are covered by an insurance provider. Dental insurance will often only cover a percentage of the individual's dental costs depending on the type of procedure performed and most plans will only cover the individual's costs up to a set amount each year. Life insurance is a health and welfare benefit in which an employee's family will receive a certain amount of money in the event of the employee's death. The specific conditions to receive death benefits and the amount the family will receive from the insurance benefit can vary greatly. Vision insurance is a health and welfare benefit in which an employee receives a discount on the amount paid for eye care.

Short-term disability insurance is a health and welfare benefit providing an employee a percentage of income each month if disabled for a relatively short period of time. These plans will provide benefits to an individual that is unable to work, or for certain plans, unable to work in his or her chosen profession. It will usually provide benefits for a specific period of time, but will usually not provide benefits for a period longer than two years. Long-term disability insurance is a health and welfare benefit providing an employee with a percentage of his or her income each month if disabled for an extended period of time. Long-term disability insurance plans will provide benefits to an individual similar to a short-term disability plan except but will usually provide benefits for a period that is two years or longer.

Important terms

The following are terms associated with pay:
- Base pay - Base pay refers to the standard amount received for performing work before any special pay is added. An individual's base pay is the regular wage received per hour or the regular salary received per pay period.
- Differential pay - Differential pay is special pay added to base pay to encourage individuals to perform certain tasks they would normally be unwilling to perform. Differential pay is usually paid to employees for performing unpleasant or unusual work such as working in hazardous environments, working more than 40 hours in a week, or working overnight shifts.
- Variable pay - Variable pay, also known as incentive pay, is special pay added to base pay to encourage the achievement of goals. Variable pay is usually paid to employees meeting performance goals such a selling a certain number of products.
- Pay grade - A pay grade, also referred to as a job grade or a step, is a pay category consisting of a series of positions of similar value.
- Pay range - A pay range refers to a set of base pays equal to or greater than the minimum base pay and less than or equal to the maximum base pay an individual can typically earn for a particular pay grade.
- Pay range spread - A pay range spread refers to a percentage used to describe the size of a specific pay range. A pay range spread can be determined by using the formula: (maximum – minimum) / minimum = spread.

- Annual review - An annual review is a yearly evaluation of an individual's pay where decisions are made regarding additional pay for performance or seniority. There may be a percentage raise based on a performance system or a seniority system that assigns a specific increase based on the individual's time with the organization.
- Cost of living adjustment - A cost of living adjustment, also known as a cost of living increase, is an automatic pay increase for changes related to inflation or increases in local costs. A cost of living adjustment is usually a flat percentage increase added to each employee's pay.

Employee and Labor Relations

Employee relations

The term employee relations refers to how an organization interacts with its employees and the methods used to build and maintain relationships between employees and other individuals outside the organization. It is important to be concerned about employee relations for two primary reasons. First, it is difficult for an organization to function normally if decent relationships cannot be maintained between employees and customers, employees and vendors, employees and managers, etc. This is because employers having difficulty establishing decent relationships with employees will usually have difficulty encouraging individuals to join the organization, to stay with the organization, and motivating individuals within the organization to perform up to or beyond expectations. Secondly, there are legal concerns associated with an organization's employee relations because certain practices may violate federal, state, or local laws and may subject the organization to liability.

Constructive discharge

The legal concept known as constructive discharge refers to a common law protection offered by certain states holding an employer responsible for the work environment. It holds an employer responsible if an individual terminates employment because the employer has created a hostile work environment. A constructive discharge is a situation in which an employer creates a work environment that is so threatening and ultimately unpleasant the individual has no choice but to terminate employment. The specific requirements a situation must meet for an individual to claim a constructive discharge varies from state to state, but a lawsuit can be brought against a former employer when victims perceive and can prove the conditions existed.

Defamation

The legal concept known as defamation is a common law protection that holds an employer responsible for any communication that unfairly affects an individual's reputation. It holds an employer responsible if an individual is adversely affected by a statement made by the employer through any medium if that statement is untrue or unrelated to the individual's performance. If an employer lies or releases information completely unrelated to an individual's ability to perform a task, such as the individual's sexual orientation, and that information prevents the individual from receiving a specific benefit, such as a position with another organization, the employer may be held liable for any damage caused by the false or unrelated information.

Employment-at-will

The legal concept known as employment-at-will is a common law protection allowing an employer or an employee to terminate an employment agreement at any time. This common law allows an employee to terminate employment at any time for any reason and allows an employer to terminate the employee's employment at any time for any reason as long as the individual is not terminated in violation of any other employment law or public policy. However, it is also important to note that the employment-at-will protection may not apply if there is a contract between the employee and the employer that would prevent the termination or if there is a policy established by the employer that would prevent the employer from terminating the employee without going through a specific procedure first.

Contracts

The two main types of contracts that may prevent an employer from terminating an employee are expressed and implied contracts. An expressed contract is a written document created by the employer or a verbal statement made by the employer or representative establishing the arrangement existing between the employee and the employer. An expressed contract can prevent an employer from terminating an individual's employment if the contract guarantees employment or states that the individual may only be terminated under very specific circumstances. An implied contract is a written document created by the employer, a verbal statement made by the employer or representative, or an activity that the employer consistently performs that establishes a policy for the appropriate procedure that must be followed for an individual to be terminated. An implied contract can prevent an employer from terminating an individual's employment if it establishes a standard action the employer must take before terminating the employee, such as following a disciplinary process or identifying a just cause.

Good faith and fair dealing

The legal concept of good faith and fair dealing is a common law protection holding an employee or an employer responsible for upholding the agreement established by an expressed or implied employment contract. It requires each individual involved in a particular employment contract to act in a way that will allow the agreement to be carried out as agreed upon by the employer and the employee. In other words, an employee must be able and willing to perform the tasks associated with the contract and the employer must be able and willing to provide the compensation and benefits in exchange for work. An employee who lies about experience, education, skills, and other abilities or background information may be held liable for false statements and an employer who lies about the benefits the individual will receive or deliberately prevents the employee from claiming those benefits may be held liable.

Promissory estoppel

The legal concept known as promissory estoppel is a common law protection holding an employer responsible for stated promises. It holds an employer responsible when an employee is promised a particular reward in exchange for taking a particular action, but then never receives the reward. It is important to note that the protections offered by promissory estoppel are similar to those of good faith and fair dealing except that an employer may be held liable for not carrying out a promise made to an employee even if the promise was made in good faith.

Respondeat superior

The legal concept known as respondeat superior, which literally means, "let the master answer," is common law protection holding an employer responsible for the actions of employees as they are performing tasks for the employer. It holds an employer responsible for any civil offense committed by an employee while the individual is performing work for the employer if the offense is related to the employee's standard responsibilities. An employer may be held liable for any actions taken by managers, supervisors, and employees if one of these individuals commits an act that is a violation of civil law while performing his or her standard responsibilities. It is also important to note that, in certain situations, an employer may be held liable under respondeat superior even if the employer was unaware of the employee's actions.

Glass Ceiling Act

The Glass Ceiling Act, which was passed as a section of Title II of the Civil Rights Act of 1991, was originally designed to assess whether an individual belonging to a protected class would typically be able to reach a senior management position within an organization. The assessment mandated by this act, which was performed by a commission, was designed to study various organizations to determine how difficult it was for a protected individual to reach a senior management position. The assessment mandated by this act also required the commission to identify the specific causes, referred to as barriers, which prevented a protected individual from progressing towards the upper levels of the organization if the commission determined it was extremely difficult or nearly impossible.

The commission formed by the Glass Ceiling Act established that in certain organizations it was extremely difficult or nearly impossible for a protected individual to advance to a senior management position due to three different advancement barriers. The three advancement barriers are governmental barriers, internal structural barriers, and societal barriers. A governmental barrier is an obstacle that occurs because the equal employment opportunity regulations that apply to the individual are not enforced. An internal structural barrier is an obstacle that occurs because the practices, policies, programs or cultural norms within the organization make it difficult or impossible for the individual to advance. A societal barrier is an obstacle that occurs because the individual does not have access to the education required to advance or society's preconceived ideas regarding the particular protected class makes it difficult for the member to advance.

Settling discrimination charges

There are a variety of reasons an organization might want to settle a discrimination charge before the charge can be investigated by the Equal Employment Opportunity Commission (EEOC) or investigated by a state or local Fair Employment Practices Agency (FEPA.) One of most common reasons for an organization to settle a discrimination charge is to avoid the financial costs (court fees, lawyers' fees, financial obligations if the courts find in favor of the complainant) associated with defending itself. Another common reason for an organization to settle a discrimination charge is to avoid or minimize damage to its reputation. Any charge of discrimination, regardless of whether it has any basis or not, will affect the organization's reputation as employees, customers, and vendors. An organization might settle a discrimination charge to avoid media coverage or rumors that might do damage the organization's reputation, employee relations, and ultimately make it difficult to function normally.

Additionally, an organization may settle a discrimination charge to avoid the EEOC or FEPA investigation itself. An organization can avoid devoting time or resources associated with providing the information necessary for the investigation by settling the charge before the investigation begins. It is also important to note that, in certain situations, an organization may also wish to avoid an investigation because it has actually committed unlawful discrimination or believes an individual or group may have committed unlawful discrimination. As a result, the organization may want to avoid an investigation that will only reveal additional information about questionable activities.

Front pay

In most cases, an employer will not be required to provide an individual with front pay, but will instead be required to offer the individual the opportunity to take or return to a specific position or required to offer the individual another similar remedy if the court decides that the employer has committed unlawful discrimination. However, there are three specific situations a court may award a complainant front pay. The first situation is if the original position or a similar position is no longer available. The second situation is if the employer has shown a consistent pattern of discrimination and has made little or no attempt to eliminate the activities leading to the discrimination. The third and final situation is if the individual would be subjected to an ongoing hostile work relationship with the employer.

Organizational climate and culture

Organizational climate is the perception of individuals and how those perceptions affect the feelings about the organization of each individual. It refers to how each employee feels about his or her work environment and the organization as a whole. It can be an important factor to monitor in any organization because the way employees feel can greatly affect the ability of the organization to retain and motivate employees. It can often be difficult for an organization to control climate because of the number of factors affecting perception.

An organization's culture and an organization's climate are very closely related, but are separate. Culture refers to the beliefs and values the employees and managers of an organization have established and the way those individuals act based on those beliefs and values. Climate refers to the way individual's perceive and feel about the organization. Organizational culture refers to the work environment the members of the organization have created and climate refers to how the members of the organization feel about that environment.

Encouraging communication and involvement

It is possible for a particular strategy to be used as both a communication strategy and an involvement strategy because, in many situations, the amount of employee involvement within an organization is closely related to the amount of employee communication. Strategies encouraging communication between employees and management will often allow employees to have more input in decision-making and ultimately allow employees to become more involved in operations as a whole. However, this does not necessarily mean that every strategy is both a communication strategy and an involvement strategy. In fact, a strategy allowing a manager to communicate important information to employees without allowing each employee to respond to or discuss the information may be considered a communication strategy, but it cannot be considered an involvement strategy. At the same time, a strategy allowing an individual to have more control over a particular task may be an involvement strategy without being a communication strategy, as it does not necessarily encourage an individual to communicate.

Involvement strategies:
- Delegating authority refers to an employee involvement strategy in which an organization grants an individual the power to make decisions related to position. This strategy allows an individual to become more involved in the organization by allowing certain decisions to be made without receiving permission.

- An employee survey, also known as a climate survey, is an employee involvement strategy in which an organization gathers information about the priorities and concerns of employees by having them fill out and submit a form.
- A suggestion program is an employee involvement strategy in which an organization gathers ideas about how to control or eliminate problems by allowing employees to submit anonymous ideas. Suggestion programs usually use suggestion boxes, voice mail, etc.
- A committee, in this context, is a group of employees within an organization who work together to make decisions related to a particular concern of the organization. Employees may be assigned to a committee temporarily or permanently depending on the concern or activity the committee is designed to handle.
- An employment-management committee, also referred to as an employee participation group, is a group of employees who work with the supervisors and managers to make decisions related to a particular concern. Employees, supervisors, and managers may be assigned to an employment-management committee temporarily or permanently, depending on the specific concern or activity the committee is designed to handle.
- A task force is a group of employees who work together to determine the cause of a particular problem and identify a solution to the problem. Employees are usually assigned to a task force until the cause of a particular problem is solved.

Communication strategies:
- A brown-bag lunch program is an employee involvement strategy in which an informal meeting is organized to discuss various concerns and issues. Brown-bag lunches are usually organized to take place during lunch to allow managers and employees to discuss issues and concerns in a relaxed setting.
- A department meeting is a formal gathering in which the employees, supervisors, and managers of a particular department discuss the various concerns and issues affecting that particular department. Department meetings usually take place on a regular basis.
- Town hall meetings, also known as all-hands staff meetings, are formal meetings in which all of the employees, supervisors, and managers within an organization attend a formal assembly to distribute important information about the organization. Town hall meetings are usually conducted in a similar fashion to a large lecture and may or may not allow for effective two-way communication.
- An open-door policy is an employee involvement/communication strategy in which employees are encouraged to share information or suggestions with managers or supervisors by assuring them they will not be adversely affected by what they say. Open-door policies are designed to establish effective communication between managers, supervisors, and employees by removing barriers preventing or discouraging the discussion of important issues with supervisors or managers. The primary advantage of an open-door policy is that it allows the organization to identify problems and solutions that may have gone unnoticed without information from employees. One disadvantage is that in certain situations a manager or supervisor may need to release information that will adversely affect an employee to handle an issue that has been reported.
- The Management by Walking Around (MBWA) strategy is simply a communication and involvement method in which an organization encourages employee communication and involvement by making managers and supervisors readily available by walking around to check on the progress of each employee, discuss questions or concerns, and handle any problems the employee or the manager identifies. This strategy is straightforward and obvious because most managers and supervisors are required to monitor employees. However, managers and supervisors need to be reminded to "manage by walking around"

because it is very easy get caught up in other activities and miss important issues that should have been identified and handled.

Communication types

There are advantages and disadvantages to each type of communication. The primary advantage of e-mail is that an organization can use e-mail to communicate important information to a large group of employees very quickly and very easily. However, the ease with which an individual can send an e-mail can also be a major disadvantage. E-mail communications make it more likely for individuals to flood the communication channels with unnecessary information or even accidentally send confidential information to the wrong people.

The primary advantage of an organization's intranet is that it allows each individual to have access to important information (such as the organization's goals, policies, practices, and updates) without allowing individuals outside the organization to have access. The major disadvantages of an intranet is that individuals outside the organization cannot access the information if they need to and the communication established is usually one-sided unless there is some other means of obtaining employee feedback.

The primary advantage of an organizational or departmental newsletter is that it can provide a lot of information about a variety of activities, issues, and concerns taking place within the organization in a single communication. However, newsletters typically require a lot of time to create and will usually establish one-sided communication unless the group writing the newsletter obtains information from employees and uses that information to write sections of the newsletter.

The primary advantage of word of mouth is that a specific piece of information can be spread very quickly from employee to employee and each employee can discuss and consider the information. The major disadvantage to spreading information via word of mouth is that each individual will usually perceive or say the same information in a different way so the meaning of the information will usually change as it spreads. As a result, as more and more people discuss the information, the information being conveyed will change until it may be very different from the original message.

Progressive discipline

Progressive discipline refers to a discipline system in which an organization modifies its response to a particular behavioral issue based on the severity of the issue and how often the issue has occurred in the past. In other words, progressive discipline refers to a process in which an organization identifies a particular behavioral problem, assesses the severity of the problem, determines whether or not the problem has occurred before, and takes a specific disciplinary action based on the organization's assessment. As a result, the primary purpose of this system is to create different responses for different situations. This can be extremely important because each situation is different and two separate behavioral problems may require two completely different responses if the two problems affect the operations of the organization in different ways. Progressive discipline addresses this need for varying disciplinary responses by allowing an organization to make sure that a response to a particular behavioral problem is not overly severe and that repeat offenders are punished more severely than first-time offenders.

The specific disciplinary stages an organization will use in a progressive discipline system can vary greatly. However, most organizations use a five-stage disciplinary process. The first stage is the coaching stage in which the behavioral issue is discussed with the individual. A first stage response

- 80 -

is usually used if the issue is relatively minor or if the issue is the individual's first offense. The second stage is the first warning stage, also known as the counseling stage, in which the organization will issue a verbal warning regarding the undesirable behavior. The third stage is the second warning stage, also known as the formal warning stage, in which the organization will issue a written warning to the individual regarding the undesirable behavior. The fourth stage is the disciplinary action stage in which the organization suspends the individual. The fifth stage is the termination stage in which the organization terminates the individual's employment.

Behavioral issues

There are a variety of behavioral issues an organization may need to address at some point. Two of the most common are absenteeism and insubordination. Absenteeism is a behavioral issue in which an employee takes excessive sick leave. This can be a major problem because individuals who regularly call out of work will not be able to perform the tasks and responsibilities that must be performed for the organization to continue functioning. Insubordination is a behavioral issue in which an employee disrespects and/or disobeys a supervisor or manager. This can also be a major problem for an organization because individuals that cannot follow instructions will make it difficult or impossible for the organization to achieve its goals.

Most behavioral issues can be addressed by creating a policy that identifies the undesirable behavior, provides an in-depth definition of which actions should be considered part of that undesirable behavior, and provides an in-depth explanation of the disciplinary action that will be taken if an individual takes one of the actions described in the policy. In the case of absenteeism, an organization should establish a clear absentee policy informing members of exactly how much sick time is allowed, the appropriate manner in which to use that sick time, what uses will be considered excessive or inappropriate, and the action that will be taken if an individual is absent on a regular basis. In the case of insubordination, a code of conduct defining certain general behaviors that are unacceptable may be sufficient to handle these issues.

Arbitration

The two main types of arbitration are compulsory and voluntary. Compulsory arbitration is a form of arbitration in which two or more parties involved in a dispute are required by law to seek arbitration. It is usually the result of a specific clause in a contract or the result of a court order. Voluntary arbitration is a form in which two or more parties involved in a particular dispute seek arbitration to solve the dispute before it goes to court. Voluntary arbitration usually occurs because the parties involved cannot come to an agreement, but all of the parties involved would like to avoid investing the time and money required for a lawsuit.

The two main types of arbitration decisions that may result from a particular arbitration are binding and non-binding. A binding decision is one in which the parties involved in a particular dispute are legally required to accept the arbitration decision and to take any specific actions, such as paying remedies, required by the decision. Once a binding decision is made, the decision is final and no party involved in a binding arbitration decision can take any further legal action based on the specific dispute covered in the decision. A non-binding decision, on the other hand, is a decision in which all of the parties involved in a particular dispute are not required to accept the arbitration decision and each party may decide to take or decide not to take the specific actions required by the decision. As a result, a non-binding decision is merely the opinion of the arbitrator regarding how the particular dispute should be resolved and any party involved in the dispute may take further legal action.

The three main types of arbitrators are permanent, ad-hoc, and arbitrator panels. A permanent arbitrator is a person who regularly handles the arbitration for any disputes that arise between certain parties. A permanent arbitrator may be part of an independent professional organization offering arbitration services or may be an independent professional that all the parties involved in a particular business relationship have agreed to use. An ad-hoc arbitrator is an individual chosen by the parties involved in a particular dispute for the sole purpose of handling that specific dispute. An ad-hoc arbitrator may be part of a professional arbitration organization, an independent arbitrator, or may be any other individual that both parties agree is impartial. An arbitrator panel is a group of arbitrators that have been chosen by the parties involved in a particular dispute for the sole purpose of handing that specific dispute. Arbitrator panels usually consist of three arbitrators and are therefore often referred to as an arbitral tribunal or a tripartite arbitration panel.

Mediation process

In most cases, the mediation process begins with the parties involved choosing an independent and impartial mediator. The mediator establishes the format of the mediation process by answering questions such as what is being disputed, who is actually involved in the dispute, when and where the negotiations will take place, and how the negotiations will be conducted. Once the format of the mediation process has been established, the parties involved in the dispute will meet, the mediator will explain the format and the purpose of the meeting, and the parties will present information related to each side of the dispute. After all of the parties involved have presented the facts related to the dispute, the mediator will attempt to help each party identify solutions to the dispute and come to a compromise. Finally, each party will sign a written document agreeing to the compromise if one is reached.

Constructive confrontation

Constructive confrontation, which was originally designed by Guy Burgess and Heidi Burgess, is a mediation method designed to address complicated disputes in which all of the parties involved are unwilling to consider alternative solutions. This method assumes that most disputes that seem to be irresolvable may be resolved if the parties involved address the secondary issues involved in a particular dispute first and then move on to the main issues present in the dispute itself. In other words, in a complicated dispute, it is possible for factors not related to the primary issue of the dispute itself to play a role in whether or not the dispute can be resolved.

Sherman Antitrust Act

The Sherman Antitrust Act, which was passed in 1890, is designed to prevent organizations from restricting free trade. This act specifically prohibits any individual or organization from entering into a contract that would significantly restrict the ability of other individuals or organizations to trade or engage in commerce. This act also specifically prohibits any individual or organization from taking any action that would form a monopoly and grants the courts the authority to issue injunctions to halt actions that would allow a particular individual or organization to monopolize a particular type of trade. This act applies to any organization unless there is a specific law protecting the organization from being considered a monopoly. Under this act, if a particular individual or organization is suspected of forming a monopoly, a government attorney or the district courts have the authority to initiate an investigation and take appropriate action.

Clayton Act

The Clayton Act, which was passed in 1914, explains the prohibitions established by the Sherman Antitrust Act in more detail and to establish regulations protecting certain organizations from being considered monopolies under the Sherman Antitrust Act. This act specifically defines some of the trade-restrictive activities that should be considered illegal including exclusive dealings, price discrimination, mergers, and any other similar activities if those activities actually prevent other individuals or organizations from competing. This act also establishes agricultural organizations and unions are exempt from the regulations established by the Sherman Antitrust Act and that court injunctions may only be used to settle a labor dispute if there is a threat of property damage.

Railway Labor Act

The Railway Labor Act, which was passed in 1926 and amended in 1936, prevents railroad and airline strikes from causing significant trade and transportation problems. This act specifically establishes that airline and railroad employees have the right to unionize and strike if the strike is related to a major contract dispute. However, this act requires employees involved in an airline or railroad union to seek alternative dispute resolution methods including arbitration and mediation before initiating a strike. This act also allows the President to declare a national emergency if an airline or railroad strike is significantly affecting trade and transportation within the United States. If the President declares a strike to be a national emergency, all strikers involved in that particular strike must return to work for a period of 90 days.

Norris-LaGuardia Act a

The Norris-LaGuardia Act, which was passed in 1932, protects the right to unionize. This act grants employees the right to form unions and initiate strikes. In addition to granting the right to unionize, this act also prohibits the court system from using injunctions to interfere with any nonviolent union activity and prohibits employers from forcing employees to sign "yellow-dog" contracts. A "yellow-dog" contract refers to any contract that prohibits an employee from joining a union or any contract that requires an employee to agree to be terminated if it is discovered that he/she is a member of a union or intends to become a member of a union.

NLRA

The National Labor Relations Act (NLRA), also known as the Wagner Act, is designed to grant certain rights to unionized workers or employees that want to unionize. This act reaffirms some of the protections established by the Norris-LaGuardia Act as it specifically grants employees the right to form unions and establishes that all employees covered by this act have the right to join a union and take part in union activities. This act also specifically establishes that all employees have the right to take part in any activity related to a collective bargaining process with their employer regardless of whether they are a member of a union or not. However, the regulations established by this act do not apply to employees covered by the Railway Labor Act or to employees working on a farm or for other agricultural employers. The regulations established by this act do not apply to managers, supervisors, independent contractors, immediate family of the employer, and any other individuals who may make labor decisions on behalf of an employer.

According to the National Labor Relations Act (NRLA), there are certain situations in which a strike should be considered legal and certain situations in which a strike should be considered illegal. The National Labor Relations Act establishes that a strike should be considered lawful if the members of

- 83 -

the union refuse to work because they are seeking an increase in their benefits, compensation, or are seeking an improvement related to their work environment. A strike should also be considered lawful if the members of the union refuse to work because their employer is using an unfair labor practice. A strike should be considered unlawful, on the other hand, if employees refuse to work even though they are covered by a contract with a no-strike clause, if employees refuse to work in order to assist the union in defending an unfair labor practice committed by the union, or if the actions taken by the employees during the strike can reasonably be expected to result in property damage or harm to any person.

The National Labor Relations Act (NRLA) identifies five types of employer practices that should be considered unfair labor practices. First, the NRLA establishes that it is unfair for an employer to interfere in the activities of a union or prevent employees from taking any action related to forming or joining a union. Second, the NRLA establishes that it is unfair for an employer to take any action that would allow the organization to control a union or offer special attention or preferential treatment to a particular union. Third, the NRLA establishes that it is unfair for an employer to discriminate against any employee because he or she is a member of a union or takes part in any lawful union activity. Fourth, the NRLA establishes that is it unfair for an employer to discriminate against any employee because he or she has filed charges with the National Labor Relations Board or has taken part in any investigation. Fifth, the NRLA establishes that it is unfair for an employer to refuse to bargain with a union representing the employer's employees.

LMRA

The Labor Management Relations Act (LMRA), also known as the Taft-Hartley Act, identifies a number of union practices that should be considered unfair labor practices. First, the LMRA establishes that it is unfair for a union to force an employee to join or take part in a union or force an employee to accept a particular representative. Second, the LMRA establishes that it is unfair for a union to refuse to bargain with the representative of an employer or restrict the ability of an employer to negotiate a contract and enforce that contract. Third, the LMRA establishes that it is unfair for a union to call for an employer to discriminate against employees that are not part of a particular union or that speak out against a union. Fourth, the LMRA establishes that it is unfair for a union to encourage individuals outside the organization to take part in a secondary boycott or encourage employers to enter into a hot cargo agreement. Finally, the LMRA establishes that it is unfair for a union to charge unreasonably high membership fees.

NLRB

The National Labor Relations Board (NLRB) is a federal agency that protects the right of employees to choose whether they want to be represented by a union or not and is designed to handle activities related to investigating and preventing employers and unions from taking part in unfair labor practices. The National Labor Relations Board can take a number of actions related to employer unfair labor practices including requiring employers to rehire or return positions to employees that were affected by an unfair labor practice, requiring employers to resume negotiations with a union, and disbanding unions that are controlled by an employer. The National Labor Relations Board may also take a number of actions related to union unfair labor practices including requiring unions to refund membership fees with or without interest to union members that have been charged unreasonable fees, requiring unions to resume negotiations with an employer, and requiring unions to accept the reinstatement of any employee if the union specifically discriminated against that employee.

Unions

Types

The four main types of unions are local unions, national unions, federations, and international unions. A local union represents employees for a single small organization or represents employees working for a large organization or a group of similar organizations in a relatively small area such as a section of a town, an entire town, an entire city, or possibly an entire state. A local union may be an independent union or a member of a national union. A national union represents employees from a variety of different areas throughout the United Sates and consists of a collection of local unions from a single national employer or local unions from a variety of different employers in the same industry. A federation consists of a collection of national unions that represent employees in a variety of different, but related industries. An international union represents the interests of employees from different countries.

Organizing process

In order for a union to be recognized as the official representative of a certain group of employees, the union must go through a four-step organizing process. First, a group of employees interested in joining the union or the union itself must establish that the members of the organization are interested in being represented by the union. Second, the group of employees or the union itself must have employees sign authorization cards to prove that the employees of the organization are interested in being represented by a union. Third, the union must inform the employer that the employees of the organization have requested to be represented by the union and that the union requests that the employer recognize the union as their representative. If the employer refuses to recognize the union as a representative, the union may file a petition with the NLRB. Once the union has been recognized by the employer, the fourth and final step is to have the NLRB conduct an election to confirm that the employees actually want to be represented by the union.

Picketing

The three types of picketing specifically allowed by the National Labor Relations Board while a particular union is campaigning are informational picketing, organizational picketing, and recognitional picketing. Informational picketing refers to an activity in which employees assemble or march with signs near a worksite to inform the public that the employees of the organization are not represented by a single authority that will speak on their behalf. Organizational picketing refers to an activity in which employees assemble or march with signs near a worksite to encourage other employees to support a union. Recognitional picketing refers to an activity in which employees assemble or march with signs near a worksite to convince an employer to recognize that a particular union represents the majority of the employer's employees.

The types of picketing specifically allowed by the National Labor Relations Board while a union is in the middle of a dispute with an employer are common situs picketing, consumer picketing, and double breasting picketing. Common situs picketing refers to an activity in which employees assemble or march with signs near a worksite used by both the employer the union is picketing against and other employers. Common situs picketing is legal as long as the signs make it clear there is a specific employer the union is picketing against. Consumer picketing refers to an activity in which employees assemble or march with signs near a worksite to inform the public that any products and services are being offered while there is a work dispute. Double breasting picketing refers to an activity in which employees assemble or march with signs near a nonunion worksite operated by the employer that the union is picketing against. However, double breasting picketing is only legal in certain situations.

Decertification

In certain cases, the employees of a particular organization may decide that the union acting as their official representative is not representing their interests effectively. In these cases, the employees of the organization may choose to remove the union's status as their representative through a process known as decertification. In order to begin the process, the employees of the organization must create a petition and obtain the signatures of no less than 30% of the organization's employees. Once the petition has the required number of signatures, the employees of the organization may file the petition with the National Labor Relations Board (NLRB) for review. If the NLRB determines that the petition has the required number of signatures and that the petition has not been filed within 12 months of the date that the union was certified as the representative of the organization's employees, the NLRB will hold a decertification election. If 50% or more of the organization's employees vote to decertify the union, the union will no longer be considered as a representative of the organization's employees.

Deauthorization

In certain cases, the employees of a bargaining unit may decide that the union acting as their official representative has put a security clause in place that is not in their best interest. In these cases, the employees of the bargaining unit may choose to remove that specific security clause through a process known as deauthorization. In order to begin the process, the employees of the bargaining unit must create a petition and obtain the signatures of no less than 30% of the unit's employees. Once the petition has the required number of signatures, the employees of the unit may file the petition with the National Labor Relations Board (NLRB) for review. If the NLRB determines that the petition has the required number of signatures, the NLRB will hold a deauthorization election for the entire union. If 50% or more of the union's members vote for deauthorization, the union's security clause will be considered null and void.

Collective bargaining

The National Labor Relations Act (NRLA) specifically requires any party involved in a collective bargaining process to negotiate in good faith. As a result, it is important for both unions and employers to be aware of the specific types of actions that may be considered "bad faith" activities. Bad faith bargaining activities an employer may engage in include making a proposal to employees before or without making the proposal to the union that represents those employees, encouraging employees to decertify the union or take any other action that would adversely affect the union's ability to negotiate, and making any changes in the favor of the employer to the terms and/or conditions under which the employees of the organization work while the collective bargaining process is taking place. Bad faith bargaining activities a union or an employer may engage in include hiding information related to the bargaining process, refusing to set and adhere to a reasonable time and place for the negotiations, taking any action that can be considered an unfair labor practice, etc.

The three categories that the National Labor Relations Board (NLRB) uses to describe the subjects that can and cannot be discussed during the collective bargaining process are illegal, mandatory, and voluntary. Illegal subjects are topics that cannot be discussed during the collective bargaining process. These subjects are usually related to activities specifically forbidden by law such as hot cargo agreements, clauses that prevent individuals from being employed by the organization if they do not join the union before assuming their position, etc. Mandatory subjects are topics that must be discussed during the collective bargaining process. These subjects are usually related to the basic terms and conditions of an individual's employment including the benefits, hours, regular pay, safety protections, special pay, and other similar terms and conditions related to an individual's employment. Voluntary subjects, also known as permissible subjects, are topics that the parties involved in the collective bargaining process may choose to discuss, but cannot be required to discuss. Voluntary subjects therefore include any topic not illegal or mandatory.

All collective bargaining agreements should include information related to the basic terms and conditions of employment the parties have agreed upon, the contract grievance process, the disciplinary process, and a zipper clause. The basic terms and conditions of employment such as the benefits, regular pay, and special pay that employees will receive and the hours and conditions under which employees are expected to work is an essential component of any collective bargaining agreement. The contract grievance process that will be used if there is a dispute over the terms or conditions established by a certain section of the agreement and the specific process that the organization will use to take action against employees that violate the terms of their employment should also be clearly stated. Finally, a zipper clause that clearly establishes the agreement is final and anything outside of the agreement cannot be discussed until the contract runs out is also an essential part of the agreement.

The four main negotiating strategies a union can use to negotiate with an organization during the collective bargaining process are single-unit bargaining, coordinated bargaining, multi-employer bargaining, and parallel bargaining. Single unit bargaining is a commonly strategy in which the representatives from a single unit meet with one organization at a time and focus all of their attention on the agreement for that specific organization. Coordinated bargaining, also known as multi-unit bargaining, is a strategy in which a group of separate unions each representing different employees within the organization negotiate with an organization as a group to reach an agreement that is in the best interest of everyone. Multi-employer bargaining is a strategy in which a union negotiates with several different organizations that employ members of the union. Parallel bargaining, also referred to as leapfrogging or whipsawing, is a strategy in which a union negotiates with one organization at a time and uses the agreement achieved with that organization as a model for the next organization.

The two main approaches the representatives of an organization or the representatives of a union may choose to use to negotiate during the collective bargaining process are distributive bargaining and principled bargaining. Distributive bargaining, which is also known as positional bargaining, is an approach in which a party establishes a specific objective they wish to achieve or a specific position for each issue before the negotiations begin. As the negotiations proceed, the party will then attempt to achieve that objective or defend that position whenever possible. Principled bargaining, on the other hand, is an approach in which a party identifies the issues most important to each side. As the negotiations proceed, the party will then attempt to discuss possible solutions and encourage the other party to suggest possible solutions for each issue so the union and the organization may reach an agreement that will benefit the employer and the employees.

Contract grievance
The specific contract grievance process a particular employee or union will need to go through to address a contract issue can vary greatly from agreement to agreement. However, the first step is usually for the employee or union representative to file a written or verbal complaint with a supervisor. If the supervisor offers a solution to the contract issue and the employee or union accepts that solution, then the grievance process ends. If the employee or the union considers the solution unacceptable or the supervisor does not offer a solution, then the employee or union may file a complaint with a manager. If the manager solves the issue, the grievance process ends. If the manager does not solve the issue, the employee or union may file a complaint with the organization's upper management. Finally, if the organization's upper management fails to solve

the issue, the employee or union may seek arbitration. This arbitration is usually binding and the employer and the union will therefore be required to accept the decision of the arbitrator.

Important terms

The following are important terms regarding employee and labor relations:
- Remedy - A remedy, also referred to as a relief, is the specific way an individual or organization attempts to relieve or "remedy" the effects of unlawful discrimination. It is the specific amount of money paid or the specific action taken to rectify the effects the unlawful discrimination has had upon the complainant.
- Back pay - Back pay refers to a type of remedy in which an individual or organization must pay the complainant an amount equal to what the complainant would have earned if he or she continued working for the individual or organization.
- Front pay - Front pay refers to a type of remedy in which an individual or organization must pay the complainant an amount equal to the future pay that the complainant would earn if the complainant returned to the organization.
- Employee communication strategy - An employee communication strategy is a method an organization uses to encourage employees to communicate with each other and with members of management. The specific strategy depends on the size of the organization, the importance of the information, etc.
- Employee involvement strategy - An employee involvement strategy is a method used to encourage employees to become involved in the operations of the organization. It usually refers to a specific program used or a specific action taken to allow an individual more control over decision-making.
- Compressed workweek - A compressed workweek is a flexible scheduling method in which employees are allowed to work several long shifts in a row to receive additional time off. In other words, a compressed workweek for a full-time employee may consist of four 10-hour days, three 12-hour days, or five 9-hour days during one week and only four 9-hour days during the following week.
- Flextime - Flextime is a flexible scheduling method in which employees are allowed to set their own hours as long as they report for work for a certain number of hours a week and/or report during required time periods.
- Part-time scheduling - Part-time scheduling is a flexible scheduling method in which employees are allowed to work shorter hours and/or fewer hours a week.
- Featherbedding - Featherbedding refers to an unfair labor practice identified by the Labor Management Relations Act in which a union requires an employer to keep paying employees in positions no longer necessary. Featherbedding usually occurs if a new technique or new technological advancement eliminates the need for a particular position within an organization.
- Hot cargo agreement - A hot cargo agreement is a verbal or written contract that guarantees that an employer will not trade or engage in business activities with a particular individual or organization. Hot cargo agreements are identified as unfair by the Labor Management Relations Act and are usually the result of a union's desire to prevent an employer from purchasing goods or services from nonunion workers.
- Secondary boycott - A secondary boycott is a situation in which a union encourages individuals outside the union to stop trading or engaging in business activities with a particular organization. Secondary boycotts are identified as unfair by the Labor Management Relations Act.

- Jurisdictional strike - A jurisdictional strike refers to a situation in which employees refuse to work to convince an employer to distribute or redistribute work to union workers instead of nonunion workers. Jurisdictional strikes are considered to be an unfair labor practice and are therefore illegal.
- Sit-down strike - A sit-down strike refers to a situation in which employees refuse to work, but also refuse to leave the worksite owned and/or operated by the employer. Sit-down strikes are prohibited by the National Labor Relations Board.
- Wildcat strike - A wildcat strike refers to a situation in which employees refuse to work even though they are working under a contract with a no-strike clause. Wildcat strikes are considered to be an unfair labor practice and are therefore illegal.
- Work slowdown - A work slowdown refers to a situation in which employees do not actually stop working, but instead deliberately work more slowly so the organization continues functioning, but not effectively. Work slowdowns are also prohibited by the National Labor Relations Board.
- Fair employment practices agency - A fair employment practices agency (FEPA) is a state or local organization that enforces anti-discrimination laws and regulations within the state or local area that the organization is located.
- Charge - A charge, in terms of equal employment opportunity, is a formal discrimination claim filed with a FEPA and/or with the Equal Employment Opportunity Commission (EEOC.) It is important to note that a FEPA, in certain situations, may file a charge with the EEOC while continuing to investigate the charge if the alleged discrimination is a violation of both state and federal law. In certain situations, the EEOC may also file a charge with a FEPA while continuing to investigate the charge if the alleged discrimination is a violation of both state and federal law.
- Complainant - A complainant or charging party is an individual claiming to be a victim of an act considered discrimination by law.
- Respondent - A respondent is the individual or party accused of committing an act considered discrimination by law.

Risk Management

OSHA

The Occupational Safety and Health (OSHA) Act that was passed in 1970 protects employees from the need to work in unsafe or unhealthy environments. This act specifically establishes a government system for setting the health and safety standards an employer is legally required to meet for a work environment to be considered safe and healthy. This act also establishes that it is the responsibility of the employer to ensure that each employee is working in an environment in which there are no apparent hazards that may lead to the employee's injury or death. In addition to these regulations, this act also establishes specific regulations regarding the appropriate practices, procedures, and standards that employees must use or meet to safeguard their own health and safety.

Record keeping and reporting

There are a series of record keeping and reporting actions an employer must take to comply with the regulations established by the Occupational Safety and Health Administration (OSHA.) First, any employer covered by the record keeping regulations established by OSHA must record and keep information on file about any work-related injury or illness. Second, any employer covered by these regulations must keep an accident report log including information that may be provided to an employee or an employee representative upon request. Third, any employer covered by these regulations must file an OSHA report for any accident that results in the death of an employee or the hospitalization of at least three employees within eight hours of the accident. Finally, employers are required to allow employees to make reports to OSHA offices regarding OSHA violations without fear of retaliation. The record keeping regulations established by OSHA apply to any employer with more than 10 employees unless that employer is in an industry specifically identified as "low-risk."

Form 300

An employer covered by OSHA is required to record information about any work-related employee illness or injury. In order to record and report this information, an employer must complete OSHA Form 300, OSHA Form 300A, and OSHA Form 301. OSHA Form 300, which is also known as the Log of Work-Related Injuries and Illnesses, is the form that an employer should use to record each work-related injury or illness. This form requires an employer to provide information about the type of injury or illness, the cause of the injury or illness, information that can be used to identify the individual that was actually injured or became ill such as the individual's name or a case number if privacy is a concern, the location at which the injury or illness occurred, and the time and date at which the injury or illness occurred. This form must be filled out within seven days of the time the employer is made aware of the incident.

Form 300A

An employer covered by OSHA is required to record information about any work-related illness or injury. In order to record and report this information, an employer must complete OSHA Form 300, OSHA Form 300A, and OSHA Form 301. OSHA Form 300A, which is also known as the Summary of Work-Related Injuries and Illnesses, is a form designed to summarize the injuries and illnesses that have occurred at a particular worksite during a single year. This form requires an employer to provide information about the total number of work-related injuries and illnesses that occurred during the previous calendar year, the type of work-related injuries and illnesses that occurred during the previous year, the number of times each type of work-related injury or illness has occurred during the previous year, and the number of days employees were out of work due to work-related injuries or illnesses. This form must be posted in a location that is easily viewable by employees by February 1st each year and remain posted until April 30th each year.

Form 301
An employer covered by OSHA is required to record information about any work-related illness or injury. In order to record and report this information, an employer must complete OSHA Form 300, OSHA Form 300A, and OSHA Form 301. OSHA Form 301, which is also known as an Injury and Illness Incident report, is a form an employer must use to describe a specific work-related injury or illness in more detail than the employer is required to provide on OSHA Form 300. This form requires an employer to provide information about the physicians and facilities that treated the employee's injury or illness as well as detailed descriptions of the employee's actions before the incident, the type of injury or illness, the specific cause of the injury or illness, and information that can be used to identify the individual that was actually injured or became ill. This form must be filled out within seven days of the time the employer is made aware of the incident.

Situations not considered work-related
An employer is not required to record any injury or illness not work-related so it is important for an employer to be aware of the specific situations in which an injury or illness is non-work-related. An incident should be considered non-work-related if the illness or injury became apparent in the workplace, but the employee was not in the workplace to perform work, the employee's illness or injury is the result of conditions or activities outside of the workplace, or the employee was performing personal activities at the workplace before or after his or her scheduled hours. An incident should also be considered non-work-related if the illness or injury occurred because the individual was in a motor vehicle accident on company property during a commute to or from work, if the illness or injury occurred as a result of eating food or drinking beverages prepared by the employee, if the illness or injury occurred as a result of medication the individual was taking for a non-work-related illness, or if the illness or injury was deliberately self-inflicted.

Posting and training actions
There are a series of posting and training actions an employer must take to comply with the regulations established by the Occupational Safety and Health (OSHA) Act. First, any employer covered by the OSHA must inform the employees of the organization of the rights and regulations established by (OSHA) and the specific health and safety standards that apply to the employees of the organization. Second, any employer covered by OSHA must train employees to recognize and use the specific procedures that must be followed for a particular work environment to remain safe. Third, any employer covered by the OSH Act must post warning signs identifying potential hazards as required by OSHA and post an OSHA poster in a location that is visible to all employees. Finally, any employer covered by the OSH Act must train employees to use safety equipment and train employees to use tools and equipment in the safest way possible.

Employer rights
In addition to establishing a series of regulations that employers are required to follow, the Occupational Safety and Health (OSH) Act grants several specific rights to employers. First, the OSH Act specifically allows an employer the right to influence health and safety standards by writing to the Occupational Safety and Health Administration (OSHA) Standard Advisory Council or appearing at a hearing related to a specific standard or set of standards. Second, the OSH act specifically allows an employer to obtain information regarding whether a particular substance used in the

workplace is toxic or not by contacting the National Institute of Occupational Safety and Health. Finally, the OSH act specifically establishes that an employer that is covered by the OSH act may request a permanent or temporary waiver if it is impossible for the employer to meet OSHA standards in a specific situation.

Employee rights

In addition to establishing a series of regulations that employers and employees are required to follow, the Occupational Safety and Health (OSH) Act grants a number of specific rights to employees. First, the OSH act grants employees the right to report hazards at their worksite to their employer or to OSHA without fear of retaliation. Second, the OSH act grants employees the right to request an OSHA investigation if an employee's work environment is unsafe or unhealthy without fear of retaliation. Third, the OSH act grants employees the right to receive copies of records related to an individual's past injuries, illnesses, treatment, and/or the individual's exposure to potentially harmful substances. Fourth, the OSH act grants employees the right to view OSHA citations and other records related to the safety and health conditions within a particular workplace. Finally, the OSH act grants employees the right to file a complaint against an employer with OSHA if the employer discriminates against an employee because he or she took advantage of a right granted by the OSH act.

On-site investigations

In certain situations, the Occupational Safety and Health Administration (OSHA) may decide it is necessary to conduct an on-site investigation into the working conditions of a particular worksite. These investigations are usually unannounced, but each investigation will follow a set of specific procedures established by OSHA, which an employer or HR professional should keep in mind. First, a trained investigator from OSHA known as a Compliance Safety and Health Officer (CSHO) will travel to the worksite and inform the employer or a member of the employer's staff that he or she has come to perform an investigation of the worksite. Once the employer has verified that the CSHO's credentials are in order, the CSHO will inform the organization's management of exactly what is being investigated at the worksite and why the investigation is taking place at an opening conference. The CSHO will then tour the facilities with a member of management and usually with an employee. Once the CSHO has completed his or her tour, the CSHO will then inform the employer of any violations at a closing conference.

The number of investigations OSHA can conduct at any one time is relatively limited as OSHA only has a limited number of Compliance Safety and Health Officers (CSHO) available at any given time. As a result, OSHA uses a priority system to identify which worksites should be investigated first based on the level of danger associated with the worksite. This priority system includes five levels and each priority level represents a certain amount of danger associated with the worksite. The five levels of the priority system from lowest priority to highest priority are follow-up inspections, planned or programmed high-hazard inspections, inspections resulting from employee complaints, inspections resulting from catastrophes and fatal accidents, and inspections resulting from imminent danger.

Follow-up investigations refer to any investigation conducted by a Compliance Safety and Health Officer (CSHO) to verify an employer has taken action to eliminate any health or safety violations the CSHO previously identified. Follow-up investigations are considered to be the fifth priority level, which is the lowest priority assigned by OSHA. A planned or programmed high-hazard inspection is an investigation scheduled for a particular worksite because the worksite is involved in an industry identified as extremely dangerous. These investigations are considered to be the fourth priority level, which is the second lowest priority assigned by OSHA. Investigations resulting from an employee complaint include any situation in which OSHA has received a specific complaint from an employee about unsafe or unhealthy working conditions and that employee has requested an investigation. These investigations are considered to be the third priority level, which is the mid-level priority.

The OSHA investigation priority system consists of five levels and the two highest priority levels are the catastrophes and fatal accidents level and the imminent danger level. Investigations resulting from catastrophes and fatal accidents refer to any investigation required because at least 3 employees have been hospitalized due to an accident at a worksite or at least one employee has died from an accident at a worksite. These investigations are considered to be the second priority level and are therefore given the second highest priority. Investigations resulting from imminent danger refer to any investigation required because it is likely an individual will die or be seriously injured in the near future due to the working conditions of a particular worksite. Investigations at the imminent danger level are assigned the highest priority by OSHA and are usually investigated first.

Off-site investigations

In certain situations, the Occupational Health and Safety Administration (OSHA) may decide it is necessary to conduct an off-site investigation into the working conditions of a particular worksite. OSHA may conduct an off-site investigation if the employees at a worksite do not appear to be in imminent danger of harm due to the health and safety violations that may be occurring at a worksite, the worksite is not related to an industry identified as high risk or already scheduled for an investigation, the employer does not have a history of any serious violations, and the employer has complied with any OSHA requests made prior to the complaint or report. If OSHA determines an off-site investigation is necessary, but an on-site investigation is not, OSHA will contact the employer by phone and identify the specific violation(s) that have been reported. Once the employer has been contacted, the employer has five days to mail or fax a written description of any health and safety issues identified and how the organization plans to address those issues.

Violation types

There are six different types of violations an OSHA investigation can identify: de-minimus, other-than-serious, serious, failure to abate, repeat, and willful. A de-minimus violation is a violation of a standard not currently affecting the health or safety of employees. Other-than-serious is a violation of a standard affecting the health and safety of employees, but there is no imminent danger of harm. A violation identified as serious is a violation of a standard in which there is imminent danger that an employee may be seriously injured or even killed. A violation identified as a failure to abate will be issued if the employer continues to violate a specific standard past the abatement date established by a previous OSHA investigation. A violation will be identified as a repeat violation if the employer continues to violate a standard that is the same or similar to a violation identified by a previous OSHA investigation. Finally, a willful violation will be issued if the employer has intentionally violated or ignored OSHA standards.

Penalties

There are six different types of violations an OSHA investigation can identify and each type of violation has a different penalty range associated with it. In the case of a de-minimus violation, the employer will be informed of the violation, but will not be cited for the violation. In the case of other-than serious or serious violations, the employer will receive a citation and may have to pay fines up to $7,000 per violation. In the case of a failure-to-abate violation, the employer will receive a citation and may have to pay fines up to $7,000 per day for each day that the violation continues after the abatement date. In the case of a repeat violation, the employer will receive a citation and may have to pay fines up to $70,000 per violation. Finally, in the case of a willful violation, the employer will receive a citation and may have to pay fines of $5,000 - $70,000 and the employer may be subject to additional penalties and jail time if an employee death resulted from the violation.

Standards

The following is a list of OSHA standards:

- The general duty standard is designed to hold employers responsible for the health and safety of their employees. This standard establishes the foundation for all of the other health and safety standards established by OSHA as it requires employers to take action to eliminate safety and health hazards from the workplace, requires employees to adhere to all of the rules and standards that apply to employees, and requires employers to adhere to all of the rules, regulations, and standards that apply to their particular organization.

- The hazard communication standard, also known as the employee-right-to-know standard, is designed to make sure employees are informed about dangerous chemicals in the workplace. This standard requires employers to create a written Hazard Communication Program informing employees of the presence of dangerous substances, the properties of the substance, the dangers associated with the substance, and how to avoid the dangers associated with the substance.

- The emergency action plan standard is a set procedure in place that employees should follow in order to handle and/or escape a fire or other emergency at the worksite. This standard establishes that an employer should create an emergency action plan with information such as how employees will escape the building, how the employer will make sure that all employees have left the building, what shutdown or emergency procedures must be followed to ensure that additional problems will not be caused by the emergency, and who is responsible for shutting down systems or carrying out emergency procedures. All employers are encouraged to design emergency action plans, but only employers in certain industries are legally required by OSHA to adhere to this standard.

- The exit route standard is designed to make sure there is a clear path an employee can use to escape a building or worksite in an emergency and requires employers make sure each escape route meets certain OSHA requirements.

- The specifications for accident prevention signs and tags are designed to make sure that hazards in the workplace are appropriately marked. This standard requires employers to use color-coded signs indicating the level of danger associated with a hazard by associating different danger levels with the color and size of the sign and to indicate the type of danger by the design on the sign.

- The fire prevention plan standard is designed to make sure there is a procedure in place employees should follow to prevent fires at the worksite. This standard establishes that an employer should create a fire prevention plan identifying fire hazards, procedures for avoiding fire hazards, fire prevention methods related to fire hazards present in the workplace, and actions employees should take to minimize the risk to themselves and others in the case of a fire. All employers are strongly encouraged to design fire prevention plans, but only employers in certain industries are legally required to adhere to this standard.

- The occupational noise exposure standard protects employees from the stress and hearing damage resulting from loud sounds in the workplace. This standard requires employers to measure the amount of noise in a workplace using specific procedures, and if the noise level is higher than the maximum acceptable level established by OSHA, an employer must take action to preserve and monitor the hearing of employees.

- The personal protective equipment standard ensures employees have access to the equipment necessary to protect from hazardous substances, materials, and environments. This standard requires employers to supply and maintain safety equipment, referred to as personal protective equipment, which employees can use to protect themselves from radiation, chemical burns, electric shocks, and any other similar hazards present in the workplace.
- The selection and use of electrical work practices standard requires employers to provide training and/or equipment that will help protect employees from electrical shock. This standard applies to employees who work with electrical systems.
- The sanitation standard is designed to make sure that each employee is working in as healthy a work environment as possible. This standard specifically requires an employer to maintain a work environment that is as clean and sanitary as possible for the industry the employee is working.
- The medical services and first aid standard is designed to make sure that employees have access to immediate medical attention in case of an emergency. This standard requires an employer to provide first aid supplies, make sure first aid supplies are readily accessible, and have personnel trained in basic first aid present at the worksite. The specific supplies, personnel, and other requirements a specific employer must maintain at the worksite to adhere to this standard depends on the specific industry the employer is a part of and the type of work being performed at the worksite.
- The lockout/tagout standard, also known as the control of hazardous energy standard, s employees from machinery that may operate or release hazardous substances without warning. This standard requires any employer with machinery that starts or stops operating automatically and employers with machinery that may discharge electricity, hazardous fluids, or cause other similar hazards without warning to use a safety device prohibiting the machine from operating when an employee is working on or near the machine.
- The machine guarding standard, also known as the general requirements for all machines, protects employees from dangerous machinery. This standard requires any employer working with tools identified as potentially hazardous such as saws or welding tools to use guards or electronic safety devices that will prevent or at least reduce the chance that the tool or equipment will injure an individual.
- The blood-borne pathogens standard protects employees handling bodily fluids in the workplace from infectious diseases. This standard requires employers to create a written exposure control plan identifying illnesses employees may be exposed to in the workplace, procedures employees should follow to limit or eliminate their exposure to any illnesses that may be present in the workplace, and procedures that should be followed if an employee is exposed to an infectious disease. This standard also requires employers to keep a log of each incident in which an employee is exposed to an infectious disease.
- The permit-required confined spaces standard protects employees from entering dangerous environments an individual may find difficult or impossible to escape. This standard requires employers to have a special permit if employees must enter spaces in which they may become trapped, injured, and/or killed, and requires employers to test the confined/dangerous space to make sure that it is safe prior to an employee entering the space.
- The respirator standard is designed to protect employees who work in environments with extremely poor air quality or in environments with airborne contaminants. This standard requires employers to provide respirator equipment to any employee who can reasonably

be assumed at risk of being injured, becoming ill, or dying from the condition of the air in the area at which the individual works.

- The walking/working surfaces standard protects employees from physical hazards at a worksite that may lead to accidents and injuries in the workplace. This standard requires employers to ensure any surface which employees need to walk on or work on such as floors, stairs, ladders, etc. are designed in as safe a fashion as possible and that each surface is appropriately maintained to ensure employees are unlikely to trip or fall.

MSH Act

The Mine Safety and Health (MSH) Act, which was passed in 1977, protects mine workers from unsafe and/or unhealthy working conditions. It requires employers in the mining industry to follow a set of specific health and safety standards to ensure that employees are working in the safest environment possible. This act also requires employers in the mining industry to submit to mandatory inspections as requested by the Mine Safety and Health Administration (MSHA) and requires that all surface mines receive at least two inspections from the MSHA each year and each underground mine receive at least four inspections from the MSHA each year. This act applies to all mines within the United States and miners and mine operators are required to adhere to the standards established by the MSHA and the MSH Act.

Drug-Free Workplace Act

The Drug-Free Workplace Act, which was passed in 1988, prevents drug-use in the workplace and accidents that may occur from employees working under the influence of illegal substances in organizations that receive federal funding or federal contracts. This act specifically requires each employer to establish a drug-free policy prohibiting employees from using, distributing, manufacturing, or being in possession of drugs in the workplace or working under the influence of controlled substances. Each employer must also notify employees in writing that these actions are prohibited and notify employees of the type of disciplinary and/or legal action that will be taken if an individual violates the employer's drug-free policy. It also requires employers to establish a drug-free awareness program informing employees of the problems workplace drug use can cause and identify places employees may seek help. This act applies to any individual or organization receiving federal funding and any federal contractor with at least $100,000 in contracts per year.

Needlestick Safety and Prevention Act

The Needlestick Safety and Prevention Act, which was passed in 2000, protects the safety of healthcare workers. This act requires an employer in an industry handling needles or other sharp equipment to identify and use safe alternatives to needles or other sharp devices or identify and use the safest possible needle devices available. This act also requires an employer to keep a detailed injury log of any employee injury and/or illness caused by a needle or sharp device. In addition to these regulations, this act also requires an employer to include employees using the needles or sharp devices in the organization's safe needle or sharp identification and decision-making process.

Sarbanes-Oxley Act

The Sarbanes-Oxley Act, which was passed in 2002, is designed to hold the senior executives of an organization responsible for any inappropriate or questionable financial practices. This act specifically holds the senior executives of an organization responsible for any sort of corporate accounting fraud, record tampering, or any other similar action taken by a member of the organization's management if that action conceals or alters the financial information the organization is legally required to provide to shareholders and/or the Security Exchange Commission. In addition to these anti-fraud regulations, this act also establishes higher penalties associated with white-collar crimes and requires employers to provide detailed financial reports and disclosures to the SEC at regular intervals and whenever there is a significant change in the financial status of the organization.

Risk assessment

Risk assessment attempts to identify each factor that may have an adverse effect on the organization, how likely it is for each factor to have an adverse effect, and the costs that may be faced if that factor actually affects the organization. It is an evaluation that performed to identify factors that may pose a risk to the organization and identify exactly how much risk is associated with each factor. The amount of risk associated with a particular factor is usually measured in terms of the financial cost the organization will have to pay if an adverse effect occurs and the probability that the adverse effect will actually occur in the future.

Infectious diseases

Some of the most common infectious diseases an employee may be exposed to are HBV, HIV, and TB. HBV, also known as Hepatitis B, is a disease that affects the liver, which an individual may be exposed to by a needle injury or by inappropriately handling bodily fluids so that infectious fluid enters the individual through an uncovered wound or through broken skin. HIV, also known as the human immunodeficiency virus, is an autoimmune disorder, which an individual may be exposed to by a needle injury or by inappropriately handling bodily fluids if the infectious fluid enters the individual through an uncovered wound or through broken skin. TB, also known as Tuberculosis, is a disease that affects the lungs and other organs of the body, which an individual may be exposed to through the air if an individual with TB sneezes or coughs in the general area of the healthy individual.

MSDS

A material safety data sheet (MSDS) is a written document describing a particular chemical substance, the types of hazards associated with the substance, and how an individual should protect themselves from hazards associated with the substance. These data sheets include information such as the ingredients that make up the substance, whether the substance is considered stable or unstable, the substance's chemical properties (such as how it reacts to temperature or pressure), other substances that the substance may react violently with, and the ability of the chemical to enter the body through contact, ingestion, or inhalation. Material safety data sheets are ultimately designed to inform employees of the dangers associated with a particular substance and, more importantly, how to avoid those dangers. This is important because employees who are unaware of the dangers associated with a particular substance are much more likely to be adversely affected by the substance. As a result, employers are legally required to provide a material safety data sheet for each chemical present in the workplace.

Physical health hazards

Three of the most common types of physical health hazards an organization may need to address are ergonomic, tangible, and stress. Ergonomic hazards cause an employee to become ill or injured due to repetitive or unusual motion. These hazards often lead to musculoskeletal disorders and injuries. Tangible hazards cause an employee to trip, fall, hit a solid or sharp object, or experience an accident because a particular object, workplace condition, or procedure is unsafe. Tangible hazards often lead to serious injury or even death. Stress hazards cause an employee to become ill or injured due to extreme physical or emotional stress. Individuals under extreme stress are more likely to experience anxiety, panic attacks, and exhaustion and may even develop heart conditions and other illnesses.

Stress

According to Dr. Hans Selye, there are three stages an individual will typically experience during an extended stressful situation: alarm or arousal stage, the resistance stage, and the exhaustion stage. The alarm stage is when the individual perceives there is a threat present and realizes the knowledge, skills, abilities, and physical attributes to necessary to handle that threat are not possessed. During this stage, the body begins producing adrenaline to allow the threat to be faced or escaped. The resistance stage is the second stage of the stress process in which the individual's body is forced to try to adapt to or handle the stressful situation. The final stage is the exhaustion stage in which the stress present begins to cause temporary or permanent damage to the individual's body because the individual can no longer handle the stressful situation.

The three main types of stress that an individual may experience are emotional, mental, and physical. Emotional stress is a type of stress in which mood, emotions, and ability to socially interact are affected by a perceived or real threat in the individual's environment. Mental stress is a type of stress in which an individual's ability to think clearly, an individual's memory, and an individual's ability to focus are affected by a perceived or real threat in the environment. Physical stress is a type of stress in which the body begins to lose its ability to function normally and the individual becomes more likely to become physically ill due to a perceived or real threat in the environment.

There are a variety of common signs and symptoms that may indicate an individual is suffering from the effects of extreme stress. Signs and symptoms of extreme emotional stress include anxiety, panic attacks, mood swings, depression, and personality changes. Signs and symptoms of extreme mental stress include an inability to focus, an inability to recall information, an inability to make decisions, an inability to think clearly, and excessive procrastination. Signs and symptoms of extreme physical stress include headaches, sweating, raised heart rate, teeth grinding, unexplained fatigue, and frequent illness.

The National Institute of Occupational Safety and Health (NIOSH) recognizes six factors contributing to stress in the workplace: career concerns, environmental conditions, interpersonal relationships, management style, task design, and work roles. Career concerns include any threat to an individual's employment or ability to advance within an organization. Environmental conditions refer to any physical workplace condition making it difficult to function normally, such as extreme heat, extreme cold, loud noises, and bright light. Interpersonal relationships include any threat to an individual's ability to socially interact or receive emotional support. Management style factors include any threat that causes an individual to feel uninvolved in the organization, uninformed regarding important information, or that the individual's needs are unrecognized by the organization. Task design factors include any task, practice, or procedure that regularly requires an individual to perform unusual, unpleasant, meaningless, or labor-intensive work. Factors related to work roles include any threat that may cause an individual to question his or her place within the organization.

Employee assistance programs

Employee assistance programs help employees cope with or address personal problems that may be affecting their work. These assistance programs can be designed to handle a variety of issues including family problems, financial issues, legal issues, substance abuse problems, stress, and other problems. Many organizations use employee assistance programs because they allow an organization to help employees cope with issues not directly related to their work. This is important because external issues or internal issues not directly related to an employee's work may have a large effect on the individual's ability to perform as expected. As a result, it is important for an organization to ensure each employee has access to the resources necessary to handle personal problems so the individual can continue to perform the tasks associated with his or her position in a safe and effective manner.

Health and welfare

Health and welfare programs are programs designed to help employees stay healthy by encouraging them to use healthy practices outside the workplace. These programs are primarily designed to prevent employees from becoming overweight, prevent health problems from going unnoticed, prevent employees from eating unhealthy foods, etc. These programs are also usually designed to help employees address current or developing health issues and help employees eliminate activities that may be affecting their health such as smoking. Many organizations use health and welfare programs because they allow an organization to help employees remain healthy. This is important because employees who are ill, frequently become ill, or employees that simply do not have as much energy as other employees are less likely to perform as expected. As a result, a health and welfare program can help an organization ensure its employees will remain healthy enough to perform up to and beyond the expectations of the organization.

Substance abuse

Substance abuse programs are to inform employees about the problems associated with substance abuse, encourage employees to avoid substance abuse, and help employees who have a drug problem. Many organizations use substance abuse programs because they allow an organization to help make sure that employees are not working under the influence of illegal substances. This is important because employees who use illegal substances at the workplace or frequently come to work under the influence of illegal substances are not only less likely to perform as expected, but are also much more likely to cause accidents or safety issues. As a result, these programs are primarily designed to prevent employees from using illegal drugs so the organization can ensure that employees are performing as effectively and as safely as possible.

The U.S. Department of Labor's Working Partners for an Alcohol and Drug-free Workplace initiative identifies five main elements that are necessary for an effective substance abuse program. These elements include a workplace substance abuse policy, drug tests, management/supervisor training, employee substance abuse education, and employee assistance programs. The workplace substance abuse policy is a written document that informs employees that substance abuse is strictly prohibited in the workplace and that disciplinary action will be taken against employees that violate the substance abuse policy. The drug tests included in the program should include tests that the organization can regularly perform to verify that employees are not taking illegal substances. The management/supervisor training included in the program should include activities related to informing management of the substance abuse policy and how to enforce that policy. The employee substance abuse education included in the program should include activities related to informing employees of the substance abuse policy and activities that discuss why employees should avoid substance abuse. Finally, the employee assistance program should specifically offer aid to employees with substance abuse problems.

There are a variety of different drug test programs that an organization can establish. However, some of the most commonly used drug test programs include pre-employment drug screening, pre-promotion drug screening, random drug testing, and reasonable cause testing. In a pre-employment drug screening program, each new employee hired by an organization receives a drug test prior to assuming his or her new position. In a pre-promotion screening program, any employee accepting a higher position in the organization must receive a drug test prior to assuming his or her new position. In a random drug testing program, the organization will test everyone in a specific team, department, or every employee within the entire organization without any advanced warning. In a reasonable cause testing program, any employee suspected of using illegal substances in the workplace or suspected of working under the influence of illegal substances will receive a drug test to verify or refute the suspicions of the employee's supervisors and or managers.

Security threats

There are a variety of different security issues that an organization may have to address at some point. However, some of the more common security threats that an organization may have to handle include natural disasters, technological issues, theft, and violent acts. Natural disasters include any naturally occurring event that may pose a threat to an organization such as earthquakes, fires, floods, hurricanes, lightning strikes, tornadoes, and any other similar natural disaster that may pose a threat to an organization's resources. Technological issues include any problems related to modern equipment or technological systems that may pose a threat to an organization such as computer viruses, identify theft, and catastrophic system failure. Theft includes any action in which the resources of the organization are illegally seized by an individual within the organization or by an individual outside the organization. Violent acts include any situation in which an individual is harmed by another individual in the workplace or an individual inside the workplace is harmed by an individual or group outside the workplace such as in the case of a terrorist attack.

Safety and health management plans

According to OSHA, there are four characteristics a safety and health management plan should have in order to be considered effective. First, an effective plan should establish a specific system that an organization can use to identify hazards in the workplace. Second, an effective safety and health management plan should establish a training program that teaches employees to avoid hazards and teaches employees to perform tasks in the safest way possible. Third, an effective safety and health management plan should include specific procedures and programs designed to eliminate hazards that the organization identified or at least minimize the risk that a hazard will injure or kill an employee or cause an employee to become ill. Finally, an effective safety and health management plan should allow employees at all levels of the organization to be involved in the identification, prevention, and elimination of hazards in the workplace.

Emergency action plans
There is certain information that should be included in every organization's emergency action plan. In fact, all emergency action plans should explain the alarm system that will be used to inform employees and other individuals at the worksite that they need to evacuate, should include in-depth exit route plans that describe which routes employees should take to escape the building, and should include in-depth plans that describe what actions employees should take before evacuating such as shutting down equipment, closing doors, etc. All emergency action plans should also include detailed systems for handling different types of emergencies and a system that can be used to verify all employees have escaped the worksite.

Fire prevention plans

There is a variety of different information that should be included in a fire prevention plan and the specific information included in a fire prevention plan will vary from organization to organization. However, certain information should be included in every organization's fire prevention plan. In fact, all fire prevention plans should provide detailed descriptions of the specific areas in which employees can find fire extinguishers and other similar fire prevention equipment, detailed descriptions of the types of fire hazards present in the workplace, and detailed descriptions of the appropriate procedures that should be followed to avoid these fire hazards. Fire prevention plans should also provide detailed descriptions of any hazardous waste that may be a fire hazard and the appropriate way to dispose or store hazardous waste to avoid a fire.

Business continuity planning

Business continuity planning is a process in which an organization attempts to ensure the organization will be able to continue functioning even after an emergency. This type of planning is important because there are a large number of emergencies that an organization can face and each one may impact the ability of the organization to continue functioning normally. As a result, business continuity planning is a process that organizations use to create a plan or group of plans that will help the organization return to normal after a natural disaster or similar emergency occurs. The process of business continuity planning usually begins with an organization conducting a threat assessment such as a SWOT analysis. Once the organization has identified the threats that exist, the organization can rank those threats based on the risk associated with each threat. Finally, the organization can create a plan or group of plans that establish a system the organization can use to recover from emergencies, which the organization can continually update as threats to the organization change.

Emergency response plan

There is certain information that should be included in every organization's emergency response plan. In fact, all emergency response plans should identify the records and resources essential to the organization, identify the individuals responsible for protecting those records and resources, and describe the procedures that individuals should follow in order to safeguard the records and resources essential for the organization to continue functioning. Emergency response plans must also establish a system the organization can use to continue communicating with vendors and the public during and after an emergency.

Disaster recovery plans

Certain information should be included in every organization's disaster recovery plan. Equipment and locations should be identified that can be utilized temporarily in the event of an emergency. Also, agencies and personnel that may be able to help the organization continue functioning immediately after an emergency should be identified. It is also wise to establish a set of procedures the organization can use to bring the personnel and equipment together after an emergency. Disaster recovery plans should also identify alternative sources the organization can use to receive supplies or products if the emergency disabled the organization's normal supply chain.

Safety training programs

Most organizations can follow a series of basic steps to create an effective safety training program. First, a safety risk assessment should be conducted to determine the safety hazards present in the workplace. Then each hazard is investigated to determine if training will help eliminate the dangers associated with the hazard. If so, information can be identified that each member needs to know about the hazard and a series of training goals and objectives based on these needs can be established. Once training goals have been established, a training program can be created, implemented and results evaluated.

Privacy policies

There are two main reasons a written employee privacy policy can be important. First, a written employee privacy policy helps explain the purpose of investigations and employee monitoring in the workplace. It is important to monitor the actions of employees and investigate suspected employee misconduct to eliminate harmful behavior. Most people consider these activities to be an invasion of their privacy so it is important to make it clear that these activities are necessary and will be carried out in a fair and reasonable fashion. The second reason is that it helps protect against unnecessary liability due to employee claims of invasion of privacy. A written privacy policy makes it clear that there are situations in which privacy should not be expected.

All employee privacy policies should inform employees the organization may conduct monitoring activities and/or employee searches, identify the specific methods used to monitor employees, identify the specific types of employee actions that will be monitored, and identify the specific situations in which the organization may conduct a search of the employee's workspace or personal items. In addition, employee privacy policies should also establish the specific search procedures, the specific process to investigate misconduct detected through employee monitoring, and explain how information taken from employee monitoring will be used.

Employee misconduct investigations

The investigation process usually begins when a complaint is received or if it is determined there is reasonable cause to investigate an employee's conduct. The organization should identify exactly what is being investigated, what sort of evidence is needed to prove or disprove the misconduct, who should be interviewed during the investigation, and which questions need to be asked to gather the necessary evidence. Next, the organization can interview the person making the complaint, the individual the complaint is against, and any other employees who have relevant information. Finally, the organization can come to a decision and take the appropriate action.

ELPI

Employment practices liability insurance (ELPI) is a risk management tool used to share financial risk associated with employee lawsuits. ELPI is insurance purchased to protect against some of the legal costs faced if an employee brings a civil suit against the organization. There are many situations an employee may bring a lawsuit because of perceived rights violations and the organization will pay huge fees in legal costs, even if they win the suit. ELPI can be extremely useful in covering these unexpected costs.

Important terms

The following terms are types of health hazards:
- Environmental health hazard - An environmental health hazard is a specific dangerous element in an employee's work environment having an adverse effect on an employee's health. In other words, an environmental health hazard usually refers to a specific condition, substance, or other similar factor present at a worksite that may cause an employee to become injured or ill. Environmental health hazards are usually divided into

three categories: biological health hazards, chemical health hazards, and physical health hazards.

- Biological health hazard - A biological health hazard is a specific activity, condition, or contaminated object that exposes an employee to an infection or a disease. Biological health hazards include needle sticks, unsanitary procedures or conditions, contaminated food, etc. that may expose an employee to an infectious disease.
- Physical health hazard - A physical health hazard is a condition, design flaw, or unsafe object in an employee's work environment that may adversely affect an individual's health. Physical health hazards include extreme temperatures, poor ventilation, extreme physical stress, objects at the workplace not appropriately marked as dangerous, and other similar physical hazards that may injure an individual or cause an individual to become ill.
- Chemical health hazard - A chemical health hazard is a substance an employee handles or is present in the employee's work environment that may adversely affect an individual's health. Chemical health hazards include toxic chemicals, radioactive substances, substances that violently react under certain conditions, chemicals that studies have shown may cause cancer, and other substances that may injure an individual or cause an individual to become ill.

Practice Test

Practice Questions

1. Which of the following questions is not one of the questions that a human resources professional needs to address in a Human Management Capital Plan (HCMP) during strategic planning?
   a. Where have we come from?
   b. Where are we now?
   c. Where do we want to be?
   d. How will we get there?
   e. How will we know when we have arrived?

2. Which of the following best describes an environmental scan that might occur during strategic planning?
   a. Reviewing policy and procedures for any non-compliance with environmental regulations
   b. Analyzing indoor conditions to ensure overall employee health
   c. Collecting details that will help the company project a goal for growth and development
   d. Using research and development techniques to create an effective business plan
   e. Collaborating with the Environmental Protection Agency (EPA) for improving the company's green standards

3. Why is an understanding of the legal process so valuable for the human resources professional?
   a. Human resources professionals are the ones responsible for contacting members of Congress in the event that legislation should be proposed
   b. The business world is increasingly involved with the legislative process, and the human resources professional is a company's outside contact for legislation
   c. Understanding the legislative process is essential for small businesses to become corporations
   d. Legislation influences the relationship between employers and employees, and the human resources professional is responsible for understanding this relationship
   e. Human resources professionals are expected to function as lobbyists to Congress should legislation need to be enacted

4. After several months of meetings, the owners of Pearson Fishing Service, an oilfield service company, have agreed on an idea affecting employee health benefits. They believe their concept should be submitted to become a congressional bill. Janice, who is their human resources professional, has participated extensively in the meetings, so the company owners ask her to advise them on the necessary steps to submit the idea. Which is the first step that must be taken for an idea to be presented as a bill to Congress?
   a. Submit the idea to the House of Representatives for review
   b. Submit the idea to a senator or representative from the congressional district
   c. Present the idea to a congressional committee for discussion
   d. Acquire signatures from a statewide petition in order to demonstrate the importance of the idea
   e. Present the idea to a congressional hearing to see if it passes review

5. Which of the following legislative acts do not provide protection for whistleblowers (employees who choose to speak out against corrupt business practice)?
    a. The Occupational Safety and Health Act
    b. The Foreign Corrupt Practices Act of 1977
    c. The Toxic Substances Control Act
    d. The Sarbanes-Oxley Act
    e. The Railroad Safety Act

6. Which of the following is not a step in the strategic planning process?
    a. Environmental scanning
    b. Formulating strategy
    c. Creating business plan
    d. Implementing strategy
    e. Making adjustments to strategy

7. Richard, who heads up a team within a large corporation's human resources department, is known for his laid-back style of management. For the most part, the team works well together and there are few problems with member interaction on the team. When a problem does arise, Richard's first impulse is to encourage the team members to work out the issue amongst themselves before he intervenes. As a result, Richard's leadership style could be described as which of the following?
    a. Democratic
    b. Coaching
    c. Transactional
    d. Transformation
    e. Laissez-faire

8. Standard human resource budget responsibilities for a company might include all of the following except:
    a. Performance increases
    b. Payroll taxes
    c. Travel expenses
    d. Repairs and maintenance
    e. Employee benefits

9. The Fair Labor Standards Act (FLSA) retains a certification of age for all employees for how long?
    a. 1 year
    b. 2 years
    c. 3 years
    d. 5 years
    e. Until employee termination

10. As of July 24, 2009, the federal minimum wage was established at $7.25 per hour. Grace Clothing, a successful line of retail clothing stores located in California, will be hiring 10 new workers at minimum wage with the option for commission. California has a statewide minimum wage of $8.00 per hour, so the company owners have contacted human resources manager Edwina regarding the disparity in minimum wage pay at the state and federal level. Which statement below best quotes the policy Edwina would cite to help Grace Clothing resolve the difference?
   a. Grace Clothing is required to pay employees the lowest minimum wage of any state in the country, which is $5.15
   b. When a federal minimum wage is lower than a state minimum wage, companies may use the federal minimum wage as their standard
   c. When a state minimum wage is higher than the federal minimum wage, the company is required to pay the state minimum over the federal minimum
   d. The size of Grace Clothing makes it exempt from minimum wage requirements, so the company has no obligation to follow either federal or state minimum wage
   e. The presence of commission means that Grace Clothing can lower the minimum wage that it pays workers because the commission payments compensate for the lower minimum pay

11. Which of the following best describes adverse impact in the selection of employees for a company?
   a. A selection rate among a protected class of more than 95% the selection rate of the highest group
   b. The negative impact of failing to diversify the selection rate among employees
   c. Any non-compliance with the rules pertaining to the Uniform Guidelines on Employee Selection Process
   d. A selection rate among a protected class of less than 80% the selection rate of the highest group
   e. Willful discrimination against a specific group when selecting new employees

12. Which of the following is not involved in the human resources professional's analysis of staffing needs?
   a. Create a list of necessary KSAs that will encourage company growth
   b. Develop a list of employees who might be ready for promotion
   c. Review the economic situation to consider any changes to the company's hiring policy
   d. Consider various hiring options for any open positions, as well as positions that will be open in the near future
   e. Review the results of past hiring decisions to increase the potential success of future decisions

13. Philippa the head of the marketing department of Caledonia Coffee Company is planning to post a position that will allow current employees of the company to apply before that position opens to the public. Because the posting will be internal (arranged in-house), the process will differ from that of a public posting. Philippa contacts the human resources department to find out which type of application would be best for an internal position. The best type of application for this situation would be which of the following?
   a. Short-form application
   b. Weighted employment application
   c. Long-form application
   d. Job-specific application
   e. No application is needed – interested employees should submit resumes instead

14. What are the human resources professional's primary role in assisting a department with conducting an effective interview?
- a. To offer any requested advice on preparing for and setting up interviews
- b. To choose the members of the prospective interview board
- c. To create the official list of questions that will be asked during the interview
- d. To conduct all interviews for prospective employees of the company
- e. To work with the interview board to select the right candidate for the position

15. During the course of an interview, Adrian notices that the candidate he is interviewing is wearing a religious symbol on a chain around his neck. Adrian wants to ask a question about the employee's religious affiliation. Which of the following questions would be appropriate, according to the equal opportunity laws?
- a. What church do you attend?
- b. Do you belong to any organizations that might be relevant to the position?
- c. I noticed the symbol around your neck – do you attend services regularly?
- d. Have you ever attended a religious service?
- e. What does the symbol that you're wearing around your neck represent?

16. Caspar is responsible for interviewing the candidates who have passed the first round of the application process for a new position at a large technology firm in Nevada. The first candidate that Caspar speaks to is a young woman with a strong resume and an accessible personality. Caspar is highly impressed and continues to remember the first candidate when he is interviewing the others. As a result, he rates the other candidates lower than the first, even though two of the other candidates have more experience than the first candidate and have even received several awards that she has not received. In conducting the interviews, Caspar has displayed which of the following types of interview bias?
- a. Cultural noise
- b. Halo effect
- c. Contrast
- d. Leniency
- e. Negative emphasis

17. Louisa is in the process of interviewing the prospective employees for an open position in the accounting department of a small publishing company. She has already interviewed several strong candidates, but she is looking forward to interviewing one of the candidates whose resume has struck her as showing significant potential. When this employee enters the room, however, it is obvious that he has not fully conquered his pre-interview nerves, and he stumbles through the first few questions. By the end of the interview, however, the candidate is doing well, responding articulately and living up to the potential indicated in his resume. Louisa, though, is unable to overcome her disappointment with the candidate's earlier nervousness and fails to see his improvement during the interview. Louisa is thus displayed by which of the following types of interview bias?
- a. Knowledge-of-predictor
- b. Stereotyping
- c. Recency
- d. Nonverbal bias
- e. First impression

18. The Uniform Guidelines on Employee Selection Process (UGESP) requires which two qualities in testing?
    a. Fairness and reliability
    b. Validity and disinterestedness
    c. Equality and fairness
    d. Reliability and validity
    e. Consideration and reliability

19. Why does the Uniform Guidelines on Employee Selection Process (UGESP) require these qualities in testing?
    a. To ensure the same results from all tests
    b. To avoid discrimination against protected classes
    c. To quantify the success rate for the company doing the testing
    d. To create a better standard for testing
    e. To prevent qualified candidates from being overlooked

20. The WARN Act was designed to do which of the following?
    a. Prevent massive lay-offs that disrupt the economy
    b. Provide new positions for employees that have been laid off
    c. Create government funding to support a struggling company
    d. Establish full severance pay for those who have been laid off
    e. Ensure rights for employees who have been laid off

21. Which of the following provides the best definition of organization development?
    a. Creating a mutual understanding of the values within an organization
    b. Discovering methods of strategic intervention to address problems within the organization
    c. Establishing means of employee participation in decisions that are made within organizations
    d. Creating a sense of balance between employers and their employees in a company
    e. Analyzing the various elements of an organization's makeup and reviewing opportunities for improvement

22. Which of the following is not a part of the four categories of intervention, as defined by Thomas Cummings and Christopher Worley in their book Organization Development and Change?
    a. Techno-structural
    b. Human resource management
    c. Change management
    d. Strategic
    e. Human process

23. The head of the administrative department for a major university has asked Raisa, a human resources professional at the school, for a team-building exercise that will benefit the administrative department. The administrative department is composed of employees who work closely together daily but often run into conflicts that indicate a clash of personalities. The department head hopes to find a team-building exercise that will improve the relationships among staff members in the department. Which of the following should Raisa recommend to the department head?
    a. A team obstacle course
    b. Role-playing situations
    c. Team scavenger hunts
    d. The Meyers-Briggs Type Indicator
    e. Real-life scenario re-creation

24. Which of the following elements is not a part of the ADDIE model of instructional design?
    a. Administration
    b. Design
    c. Development
    d. Implementation
    e. Evaluation

25. Eamon is a human resources professional for a large firm of attorneys, and he has been assigned the responsibility of developing an instructional method that is most suitable for the support staff at the firm. The support staff has been struggling with problem-solving issues, and Eamon has been instructed to utilize a training method that will allow the staff members to discuss problems and potential resolutions under the supervision of a third party expert. Which of the following instructional methods will be most effective for this situation?
    a. Vestibule
    b. Facilitation
    c. Demonstration
    d. Conference
    e. One-on-one

26. What is the purpose of a total rewards strategy?
    a. To plan for establishing salaries among employees
    b. To represent the employee brand as effectively as possible
    c. To assist in creating teamwork among employees
    d. To use budget for rewards in order to retain employees
    e. To recognize organizational changes as they occur

27. Which of the following is not a major factor in establishing compensation within an organization?
    a. IRS rules
    b. Employee salary history
    c. Conditions in the labor market
    d. Current economic situation
    e. Competition from other companies

28. All of the following are part of the Fair Labor Standards Act except:
    a. Minimum wage
    b. Exemption conditions for employees
    c. Work conditions for children under 18
    d. Overtime
    e. Federal service contracts

29. Which of the following best expresses the definition of benchmark positions?
    a. Common jobs within all organizations
    b. Evaluation of current jobs
    c. Review of market conditions for salaries
    d. Change in significant jobs in a company
    e. Review of value in positions within an organization

30. Arthur is an employee of a distribution company and is looking to request FMLA-approved leave for personal reasons. Arthur contacts Brad, a human resources professional at the company, to find out if he is eligible for this type of leave. Arthur has worked for the company for 9 months. What is the minimum period of time that an employee needs to work for an employer to request leave according to FMLA guidelines?
    a. 8 months
    b. 10 months
    c. 12 months
    d. 15 months
    e. 18 months

31. The Consolidated Omnibus Reconciliation Act (COBRA) requires that companies employing a certain number of people – or more – must offer a specified amount of health benefits. What is the minimum number of employees that a company must have for COBRA guidelines to be in effect?
    a. 10
    b. 20
    c. 30
    d. 40
    e. 50

32. Which of the following is not a piece of legislation that covers employee deferred compensation programs?
    a. Family Medical and Leave Act
    b. Retirement Equity Act
    c. Small Business Job Protection Act
    d. Older Worker Benefit Protection Act
    e. Pension Protection Act

33. The Health Insurance Portability and Accountability Act (HIPAA) was added to ERISA to do which of the following?
   a. Establish new guidelines for employee health insurance programs within organizations
   b. Ensure that all employers are responsible for covering minimum health conditions among employees
   c. Link ERISA to COBRA to protect any employees that are covered under COBRA guidelines
   d. Forbid any discrimination based on pre-existing health problems or conditions
   e. Ensure that retired employees maintain healthcare coverage

34. Which type of voluntary benefit program utilizes a typical pension plan in which the employer adds an established benefit to the plan when the employee retires?
   a. Benefit accrual plan
   b. Defined contribution
   c. Nonqualified plan
   d. Defined benefit
   e. Qualified plan

35. Which type of voluntary benefit plan goes beyond IRS guidelines and tends to be offered to shareholders and executives?
   a. Qualified plan
   b. Nonqualified plan
   c. Defined contribution
   d. Defined benefit
   e. Participation benefit

36. The so-called Glass Ceiling Act, which was an amendment to Title II of the Civil Rights Act of 1991, identified which three barriers to women advancing in the workplace?
   a. Internal, societal, governmental
   b. Federal, internal, societal
   c. Societal, personal, economic
   d. Personal, federal, internal
   e. Economic, governmental, societal

37. The Latin phrase quid pro quo, used to describe a type of sexual harassment that is forbidden under Title VII of the Civil Rights Act of 1964, means which of the following?
   a. Actions not words
   b. From the stronger
   c. Action follows belief
   d. This for that
   e. Limit before which

38. The National Labor Relations Act (NLRA) provides the right for employees to engage in "concerted activities for the purpose of collective bargaining or other mutual aid or protection" to which types of employees?
   a. Full-time employees only
   b. Part-time employees only
   c. Union employees only
   d. Non-union employees only
   e. All employees

39. Which of the following best defines featherbedding?
   a. When an employer ceases to do business with another employer
   b. When an obsolete job is retained to ensure an employee is not terminated
   c. When a union coerces an employee to participate in union activities
   d. When a union overcharges employees the union fees
   e. When an employer treats an employee badly for acting as a whistleblower

40. Which of the following best represents what an employer can do when employees begin to unionize?
   a. Employers may contact union leaders and forbid unionization.
   b. Employers may block employees who begin the process of unionization
   c. Employers may threaten to replace workers who choose to unionize
   d. Employers may explain problems with unionization to employees
   e. Employers are not allowed to discuss unionization with employees

41. The risk areas that the human resources professional is responsible for considering include all of the following except:
   a. Workplace privacy
   b. Legal compliance
   c. Safety and health
   d. Business continuity
   e. Labor relations

42. Which of the following best defines the purpose of a human resources audit?
   a. Reviewing the organization of the human resources department and making any necessary changes
   b. Taking stock of current compliance with labor relations laws and updating company policies accordingly
   c. Considering overall improvements that human resources can make within the company
   d. Reviewing current training programs to consider internal improvement
   e. Analyzing the organization's recruiting methods and policies

43. The Drug-Free Workplace Act of 1988 applies to which of the following types of organizations?
   a. Large corporations
   b. Federal contractors
   c. Government agencies
   d. Local businesses governed under municipal laws
   e. Academic organizations

44. Which of the following acts requires workplaces to maintain an environment that is "free from recognized hazards that are causing or are likely to cause death or serious physical harm"?
   a. Occupational Safety and Health Act
   b. Americans with Disabilities Act
   c. Drug-Free Workplace Act
   d. Sarbanes-Oxley Act
   e. Fair Labor Standards Act

45. Which of the following is not a stated category of OSHA violation?
    a. Serious
    b. Repeat
    c. Accidental
    d. Failure to abate
    e. Other-than-serious

46. The minimum number of employees that are required for an organization to complete OSHA forms is which of the following?
    a. 10
    b. 11
    c. 12
    d. 15
    e. 17

47. The Needlestick Safety and Prevention Act of 2000 requires organizations to do which of the following?
    a. Quarterly audits to check for sharp objects that could cause workplace injuries
    b. Removal of specified sharp objects from workplace due to potential for injury
    c. Listing of sharp objects recognized for having caused workplace injuries in the past
    d. Report workplace injuries from sharp objects, pay a fine, and provide worker's compensation
    e. Report workplace injuries from sharp objects and consider replacement object to prevent future injuries

48. Which of the following steps is not a part of the human resources professional's role in observing the guidelines of the Americans with Disabilities Act when an employee requests ADA accommodation?
    a. Request that the employee acquire medical certification of condition
    b. Meet with department supervisor to discuss employee accommodation
    c. Set up and mediate meeting between supervisor and employee
    d. Provide for all employee accommodation requests to ensure continued employment
    e. Send full review of accommodation process to upper-level management

49. OSHA requires that organizations develop three types of plans that will ensure employee protection. Two of these types of plans include an injury and illness prevention plan and an emergency response plan. Which of the following represents the third type of plan?
    a. Drug prevention
    b. Fire prevention
    c. Environmental protection
    d. Clean air
    e. Terrorism response

50. Which of the following is a necessary part of the three plans that all organizations must develop?
    a. Company policy about employee protection
    b. Disaster recovery
    c. Hazard assessment
    d. Union policy for employee protection
    e. Fellow servant rule

51. Which of the following is not a part of the due diligence process that a human resources professional must review during a merger?
   a. Affirmative Action plans
   b. Employment contracts
   c. Whistleblower prevention
   d. OSHA compliance
   e. Union activity

52. What is the human resource professional's strategic role in organizations within a company or corporation?
   a. Produce definitive change
   b. Encourage employees in their personal strengths
   c. Manage relationships between employees and the company
   d. Handle any issues arising from compliance problems
   e. Manage all employee problems

53. Which of the following does not represent steps in Enterprise Risk Management (ERM)?
   a. Identify risks
   b. Identify those responsible for risks
   c. Identify mitigation options for risks
   d. Make decisions about dealing with risks
   e. Reduce risks

54. Harold, the head of the human resources department for a large industrial machine manufacturing company, has discovered an issue that requires ERM, or Enterprise Risk Management. Upon review of important employee documentation, he has found out that that required forms are not being completed, placing the human resources department at the risk for non-compliance with federal guidelines. Using the guidelines of ERM, what should Harold consider doing to prevent further non-compliance?
   a. Terminate the employee responsible for failing to ensure correct documentation
   b. Create a new department within the human resources department that keeps an eye on completing the documentation
   c. Contact the federal agency responsible for documentation and request a reprieve
   d. Establish quarterly reviews of the documentation to ensure that it is completed as required
   e. Create a series of checklists that will make certain all company documentation is complete and up to date

55. Which of the following end results represents a way that a human resources professional can measure how the HR department is bringing value to a company?
   a. A reduced number of lawsuits against a company
   b. Increased expense within the human resources department
   c. An increased number of employee complaints indicating corporate problems
   d. The addition of new employees to the human resources department
   e. A reduced level of outsourcing from a company

56. Which motivational theory resulted in the idea that job enrichment can improve the overall quality of work and the workplace for employees?
  a. Herzberg Motivation/Hygiene Theory
  b. Alderfer ERG Theory
  c. Adams Equity Theory
  d. Skinner Operant Conditioning Theory
  e. Vroom Expectancy Theory

57. Which of the following motivational theories explores two different managerial approaches: providing rigorous structure and supervision because employees are only working for financial reward versus providing an atmosphere conducive to dialogue, growth, and modification of structure because employees work not just for financial reward, but the betterment of themselves and others?
  a. Maslow Hierarchy Theory
  b. Skinner Behavioral Theory
  c. McGregor X and Y Theory
  d. McClelland Acquired Needs Theory
  e. Adams Equity Theory

58. Which motivational theory focuses on the ability to alter behavior through intervention options, such as positive or negative reinforcement?
  a. Alderfer ERG Theory
  b. Skinner Operant Conditioning Theory
  c. Maslow Hierarchy Theory
  d. Vroom Expectancy Theory
  e. Herzberg Motivation/Hygiene Theory

59. Abbey, the head of the human resources department for a book distribution service, accidentally discovers information about one of the company employees. She learns that the employee has a genetic disease that could potentially affect the employee's ability to continue in the job. According to the Genetic Information Nondiscrimination Act of 2008, all employee genetic information is private, and companies are not allowed to locate or make decisions based on employee conditions. Now that Abbey has discovered this information, what is her responsibility?
  a. Abbey is required to report the information to her superiors, but they will not be allowed to alter the employee's work situation
  b. Abbey must inform the Department of Labor about her inadvertent acquisition of the knowledge
  c. Abbey must let the employee know what she has discovered and counsel the employee to consider requesting a change in the employee's job situation
  d. Abbey must place the information in the employee's company file, but it cannot be accessed unless absolutely necessary
  e. Because the information was gained accidentally, Abbey is not legally responsible for it, but she is not allowed to divulge any of the information or change the employee's working situation

60. According to Marcus Buckingham and Curt Coffman in First, Break All the Rules, which of the following is not one of the four factors that help to create eager and content employees?
   a. Terminate employees who fail to connect with other members of the team
   b. Create clear goals for all employees and provide rewards for completed goals
   c. Focus on the strengths of each employee and encourage individual growth
   d. Identify potential employees who demonstrate versatility and a combination of KSAs (knowledge, skills, and abilities)
   e. Locate the most advantageous work situation for each employee

61. What is the purpose of the Training Adjustment Assistance (TAA) program?
   a. To create funding for employees who have been terminated for any reason
   b. To help employees who lose their jobs due to a rise in the number of imports
   c. To establish health benefits for employees after they have been laid off
   d. To improve the quality of employee working conditions
   e. To work in coordination with the welfare system to support employees

62. Gabriela is a human resources professional who has been given the responsibility of filling a position within the HR department. She is ready to begin making the details of the position available to interested candidates and pursuing potential employees who will fill the requirements of the job as best as possible. This process is known as which of the following?
   a. Hiring
   b. Sourcing
   c. Tracking
   d. Selection
   e. Recruiting

63. During succession planning, a human resources professional may categorize employees as all of the following except:
   a. Employees who are ready for a new position on the company
   b. No employee is necessary because the position is now obsolete
   c. Employees who show indications that he or she is ready for a promotion
   d. Employees who fulfill all of the requirements of the position
   e. Employees who are expected to or will be required to leave the position soon

64. Eric is in charge of interviewing candidates for an open position in a hotel chain. As he considers each candidate, he finds himself quick to write off one young man in particular. This candidate has a strong resume and excellent credentials, but Eric decides that he just does not like this person and is disinclined to consider him a contender for the position. In doing so, Eric is demonstrating which of the following interview biases?
   a. First impression
   b. Cultural noise
   c. Gut feeling
   d. Leniency
   e. Nonverbal bias

65. Jocelyn has the responsibility of interviewing the candidates who have applied for an open position as a mechanic in an auto repair shop. As she meets and interviews the various candidates, she is not pleased with the potential employees that she encounters during this interview. One of the candidates, however, is a strongly built young woman with a tough demeanor. Despite this woman's limited resume and experience, Jocelyn decides that this particular candidate is the best employee choice because her appearance fits the image that the auto repair shop will need. In this, Jocelyn is demonstrating which of the following interview biases?
   a. Stereotyping
   b. Similar-to-me
   c. Recency
   d. First impression
   e. Gut feeling

66. Which of the following is the best definition of an employee brand?
   a. The public relations strategy for a company's success
   b. The human resources policy of marketing the company to prospective employees
   c. A clear portrayal of the company's identity
   d. The total rewards philosophy for a company
   e. The logo that represents a company

67. A data management company is looking to hire several new candidates who will be responsible for researching current data and cleaning up outdated files within the database. The database clean-up will cover four separate departments within the company, so the new employees will be required to work with the heads of each of the department. Lydia, who is the human resources professional for the company, has been asked about which type of interview would be most effective for this position. Considering the job situation, what type of interview should Lydia recommend?
   a. Panel
   b. Behavioral
   c. Patterned
   d. Stress
   e. Nondirective

68. How do conditions in the labor market affect a company?
   a. Ability for a company to consider and hire the right candidates
   b. Potential for negative effect on the company's bottom line
   c. Analysis of competition with other companies
   d. Geographic changes to the economic situation as a whole
   e. Changing educational expectations for potential employees

69. The Foreign Corrupt Practices Act (FCPA) was designed to do which of the following?
   a. Prevent illegal trafficking of merchandise
   b. Curtail extensive imports to bolster domestic manufacturing
   c. Maintain fair standards in American businesses that have locations abroad
   d. Prevent American businesses from bribing foreign governments
   e. Protect American workers who go to work overseas

70. A private company works as a contractor for federal defense agency. As a result of this agreement, many of the contractor employees will be engaging in positions of extreme sensitivity, and the contractor would like to give polygraph tests to employees. What is the federal policy regarding polygraph tests in this situation?
  a. All contractor employees may be given polygraph tests
  b. Federal law makes polygraphs illegal for anyone or any institution but the   government to administer
  c. The employer may utilize anyone in the company to administer the polygraph
  d. Because the contractor does other work outside of his or her work with the defense agency, polygraphs are not allowed
  e. The polygraph test may be administered only to those who will be working in defense-related jobs

71. Which of the following best defines the purpose of talent management for the human resources professional?
  a. Creating interest for potential employees and developing current employees with the potential for management and executive positions
  b. Locating new talent that will enable the organization to grow and improve
  c. Training all employees for expected promotions within the organization
  d. Setting apart employees who are currently ready or will be ready for higher positions
  e. Identifying employees who have the most potential and training them for management positions within the organization

72. Which of the following are not steps in an analysis of training?
  a. Establish a clear objective for training
  b. Collect data about potential problems and review it
  c. Analyze where the organization is lacking in its objective and its outcome
  d. Develop new and more effective training material
  e. Consider options with respect to the organization's available budget and time

73. Susannah, who is the head of the human resources department, will be responsible for a training session and must decide on the seating style in the space that she will be using. The training will include a large group and will involve a range of activities, including several lectures, film presentations, and a small amount of group work. Which of the following seating styles will be most appropriate for the training that Susannah will be conducting?
  a. Theater-style
  b. Chevron-style
  c. Banquet-style
  d. Conference-style
  e. U-shaped-style

74. Human resources professional Jacob conducts an evaluation that considers required changes and the outcome of those changes over the course of six months. Jacob begins with a written objective stated on the evaluation form and then returns to this objective at the end of the six months. Jacob is utilizing which of the following types of evaluations?
  a. Reaction
  b. Learning
  c. Pretest/Posttest
  d. Behavior
  e. Results

75. What is required in the role of the human resources professional when considering unique employee needs?
  a. Assessing the boundaries of the current policies of the organization
  b. Creating diversity initiatives by enabling employees to find a comfortable place within the company
  c. Recognizing that the most effective employees are those who are able to balance their work with situations outside of work
  d. Locating repatriation situations for employees who have the potential to benefit the organization outside the United States
  e. Establishing flexibility within the working arrangements of employees by providing daycare programs, nutrition and health training, and fitness centers

76. Which of the following best explains the primary role of fiduciary responsibility for the human resources professional?
  a. Creating unimpeachable trust
  b. Avoiding any indication of favoritism
  c. Handling the total rewards program at the organization
  d. Recognizing the need to handle sensitive material carefully
  e. Assuring a sense of trust in the organization's total rewards program

77. How are vacation pay policies established for organizations?
  a. Vacation pay policies are created under the guidelines of the FMLA
  b. Vacation pay policies are established by each company
  c. Vacation pay policies fall under the rules of ERISA
  d. Vacation pay policies fall under the jurisdiction of state-established guidelines
  e. Vacation pay policies are created by union policies within companies

78. Which of the following best explains workers compensation laws regarding an employer's responsibility?
  a. Employers are responsible for any work-related injuries or health problems
  b. Employers are responsible for any health problems that an employee develops while working for the employer
  c. Employers do not have to assume responsibility for employee problems unless the employee proves definitively that the problem is job related
  d. Employers may utilize federal aid for most work-related injuries and problems that employers develop on the job
  e. Employers are only responsible for a federally designated list of injuries and problems that employees develop on the job

79. Defined contribution plans for organizations include all of the following options except:
  a. 401(k)
  b. Money purchase plans
  c. Profit-sharing plans
  d. Cash-balance plans
  e. Target benefit plans

80. The "golden" benefits for executive compensation packages include all of the following except:
   a. Golden lifeboat
   b. Golden parachute
   c. Golden handshake
   d. Golden handcuffs
   e. Golden life jacket

81. What is the fiduciary role of the human resources professional regarding ERISA?
   a. Setting up pension accounts for employees
   b. Handling and managing pension funds
   c. Ensuring that the HIPAA guidelines of ERISA are observed
   d. Creating the rules that govern individual retirement account for employees
   e. Working with organization to locate the funds for pension accounts

82. How long after filing with the Department of Labor are ERISA records required to be maintained?
   a. 4 years
   b. 5 years
   c. 6 years
   d. 7 years
   e. 8 years

83. Which of the following pieces of legislation establishes guidelines for retaining and reporting employee identification records?
   a. Fair Labor Standards Act
   b. Fair Credit Reporting Act
   c. Consumer Credit Protection Act
   d. Small Business Job Protection Act
   e. Personal Responsibility and Work Opportunity Reconciliation Act

84. Which type of voluntary benefits plan offers specified tax benefits for employers as well as employees and does not provide extra benefits for shareholders or executives?
   a. Nonqualified plan
   b. Defined contribution
   c. Qualified plan
   d. Cash balance
   e. Defined benefit

85. Which type of voluntary benefits plan relies on unknown benefits that result from investments that are gained on the retirement account?
   a. Participation benefit
   b. Nonqualified plan
   c. Cash balance
   d. Qualified plan
   e. Defined contribution

86. Which of the following represents an occasion when picketing would be illegal?
    a. When an election for union representation has occurred within a 12-month period
    b. When employees try to provide potential customers with information about business practices
    c. When a union tries to encourage non-union employees to join the union
    d. When a union attempts to encourage the employer to recognize union representation
    e. When employees make efforts to inform the public about the employer's position regarding unions

87. All of the following represent collective bargaining strategies except:
    a. Single-unit bargaining
    b. Principled bargaining
    c. Parallel bargaining
    d. Multi-employer bargaining
    e. Multi-unit bargaining

88. Which of the following types of bargaining strategies between an employer and union employees is considered to be illegal?
    a. Double breasting
    b. Lockout
    c. Secondary boycott
    d. Common situs picketing
    e. Sit-down strike

89. An unfair labor practice (ULP) is defined as
    a. Any type of coercion on the part of employers against unions
    b. Discrimination against employees and union representatives during a strike
    c. Activity from employer or union that hinders employees from exercising rights
    d. Participating in strikes or boycotts that are prohibited by law
    e. Restraint that employers use to prevent employees from unionizing

90. During a lawful economic strike, employers have the right to do which of the following?
    a. Confront employees and require that they return to work at the risk of being fired
    b. Hire new employees to replace striking employees
    c. Encourage the union to disband or a suggest the formation of a new union
    d. Disband union bargaining and require new representation
    e. Restrict union bargaining if they negatively impact company's finances

91. Which of the following is not considered by OSHA to be a standard environmental health hazard?
    a. Ergonomic design
    b. Stress
    c. Plants
    d. Computer use
    e. Vibrations

92. Employers are legally allowed to check and review employee emails subject to which of the following requirements?
    a. Immediate notification from the legal department of impending review
    b. Evidence to suggest wrongdoing on the employee's part
    c. Written policy informing employees of potential for email searches
    d. No notification is required, therefore employers may check and review employee emails at any time
    e. Employers are not allowed to check or review employee emails without employee permission

93. The National Institute of Occupational Safety and Health (NIOSH) describes a certain workplace condition as "harmful physical and emotional responses that occur when the requirements of the job do not match the capabilities, resources, or needs of the worker." Which of the following workplace conditions does this quote define?
    a. Panic
    b. Depression
    c. Disorganization
    d. Insecurity
    e. Stress

94. Which of the following represents a legitimate reason for company management to conduct a workplace investigation?
    a. An employee is accused of inappropriate behavior toward other employees
    b. The company experiences a rapid reduction in the price of their stock
    c. Management becomes aware of a breach in legal compliance
    d. A supervisor reports a disagreement among co-workers in his or her department
    e. The human resources supervisor recognizes clear organizational problems within the human resources department

95. Risk management activities for Civil Rights are covered under which of the following pieces of legislation?
    a. EEOC
    b. SOX
    c. OSHA
    d. SEC
    e. MSHA

96. The phrase unholy trinity refers to which of the following organizational controls?
    a. OSHA logs for record of workplace injuries
    b. Top-tier leaders of the organization
    c. Steps of a human resource audit
    d. Common law doctrines for worker's compensation
    e. OSHA requirements for IIPP

97. OSHA 300 represents which of the following:
    a. Summary of Workplace Problems
    b. Injury and Illness Incident Report
    c. Log of Work-Related Injuries and Illnesses
    d. Employee Privacy Case List
    e. Record of Employee Complaints and Referrals

98. Employers will typically use which of the following in order to protect confidential company information?
   a. Lie detector test
   b. Nondisclosure agreement
   c. Employee contract
   d. Video surveillance
   e. Random searches

99. The components of an effective substance abuse program include all of the following except:
   a. A written statement regarding the company's no-tolerance policy about substance abuse
   b. Upper-level management support for all substance abuse programs and policies
   c. Educational awareness for incoming employees regarding the company's substance abuse policy
   d. Management training programs for implementing substance abuse policy
   e. Targeted drug testing for employees who have substance abuse problems

100. A large university is concerned about the possibility of an act of terrorism on campus, and the supervisor for the school's student affairs program has consulted Angelova, the head of the human resources department, about developing a program for responding to a terrorist attack and assisting students in the aftermath of an attack. Which of the following represents what Angelova could recommend to the student affairs supervisor?
   a. A counseling program that assists students in recovering from the trauma of a terrorist attack
   b. A relocation program that enables students to transfer to other schools in the aftermath of a terrorist attack
   c. A monthly email newsletter that provides recommendations for students should the school experience an act of terrorism
   d. Creation of new department specifically focused on responding to a terrorist attack on campus
   e. A school-wide emergency response program that gives students information on how to protect themselves during a terrorist attack

Answers and Explanations

1. A: A Human Management Capital Plan is forward thinking; the questions asked look at the present and into the future. As a result, a human resources professional who is setting up a HCMP should ask the following questions as demonstrated in answer choices B, C, D, and E: Where are we now? Where do we want to be? How will we get there? How will we know when we arrive? Answer choice A, which asks where have we come from, addresses an issue that does not apply to this portion of strategic planning, so it is correct.

2. C: An environmental scan has to do with the gathering of information that will help to project company growth and development. In other words, an environmental scan helps a company to review historical data to begin the process of preparing for expected or planned growth in the company. The environmental scan has nothing to do with environmental standards, federal or otherwise. This means that answer choices A, B, and E can be eliminated because all refer to outdoor or indoor environment, the EPA, and green standards. Answer choice D may be eliminated as well because the environmental scan does not relate to research and development techniques, nor is it specifically related to a business plan in the immediate sense.

3. D: Simply put, the legislation that will affect a business often will affect that business's relationship with its employees. Because the human resources professional is, in some ways, the intermediary between the employers and the employees, he or she should be at least somewhat familiar with legislation and the legislative process. Answer choice A is not correct because the human resources professional is not necessarily responsible for contacting a member of Congress about submitting legislation. Similarly, answer choice B is incorrect because the human resources professional is not required to act as the company's outside contact. Answer choice C is largely irrelevant to the larger question and, if true, would only refer to human resources professionals at small companies that are hoping to expand. Answer choice E is also incorrect because lobbying before Congress is a task that anyone can perform, but does not necessarily fall under the specific job description of the human resources professional.

4. B: Question 4 essentially asks the student to choose the first step in the legislative process for a bill to become a law. When an idea for a bill originates from an individual or business outside of Congress, the idea must first be submitted to a member of Congress (known as MOC). This MOC may be either a senator or a representative. The MOC will then sponsor the bill by submitting it to the part of Congress where he or she works, and the bill will begin its journey through legislation. Answer choice A is incorrect because no business or individual has the ability to submit a bill to either part of Congress. That obligation belongs to the MOC. Answer choices C and E are incorrect because they again overstep the boundaries of the MOC. First the MOC must sponsor the bill; then it goes into a congressional committee and/or hearing. Answer choice D is also incorrect because a statewide petition, while valuable for some processes, plays no real part in the legislative process.

5. B: The Foreign Corrupt Practices Act of 1977 establishes the rules for preventing bribery and penalizing occurrences of it within corporations that exist in several countries. Each of the other answer choices – A, C, D, and E – all provide some kind of protection for whistleblowers who reveal corrupt business practices.

6. C: Creating a business plan, while useful for businesses that are in their early stages, is not an identifiable step within the strategic planning process that a human resources professional may complete. On the other hand, completing an environmental scan (answer choice A), formulating a strategy (answer choice B), implementing that strategy (answer choice D), and adjusting the strategy (answer choice E) are all significant steps in the strategic planning process. It is important to bear in mind that strategic planning is related largely to a company's future goals for growth and improvement.

7. E: Richard's laid-back mentality demonstrates a laissez-faire, or "let it be" attitude toward managing his team in the human resources department. A democratic leadership style (answer choice A) provides plenty of freedom among team members but still maintains a sense of order and control. A leader who demonstrates the coaching style (answer choice B) has a more hands-on approach to working individually with team members to help them with targeting their skills and giving them the means to function on their own. A transactional leader (answer choice C) sets goals and provides rewards to team members as they reach these goals, while a transformational leader (answer choice D) works on team dynamics for a united approach to reaching goals.

8. A: In terms of standard budget responsibilities, the human resources professional is expected to manage payroll taxes (answer choice B), travel expenses (answer choice C), repairs and maintenance (answer choice D), and employee benefits (answer choice E). The performance increases tend to fall under human resources in some cases but are not considered standard responsibilities, so answer choice A is correct.

9. E: The Fair Labor Standards Act requires that companies maintain a certification of age on file for all employees until their employment is terminated. The certification of age simply shows that the employee can legally work for the company in the capacity in which he or she was hired. Once the employment has been terminated, it is no longer necessary to maintain a certification of age. Answer choices A, B, C, and D all represents time periods that could be true depending on the time that an employee is with a company, but they are not technically correct based on the wording of the law.

10. C: Minimum wage law is as follows: the federal minimum wage is primary if the state minimum wage is lower than the federal minimum wage. If the state minimum wage is higher than the federal level, however, the company is required to pay the state minimum wage. In other words, companies are expected to pay whatever happens to be higher. There are, of course, a number of variables that can affect minimum wage and what a company is expected to pay, but in question 10 one should assume that Grace Clothing in California is required to pay whatever happens to be the higher minimum wage. This means that answer choices A and B are immediately incorrect. In the case of answer choice D, the question does not provide any information about the size of the company, so the answer choice becomes irrelevant to the discussion. (Again, it must be assumed based on the question that Grace Clothing is required to pay minimum wage; the real question is which minimum wage?) And answer choice E is incorrect because the presence of commission should not necessarily affect minimum wage. The minimum wage is the minimum a company is expected to pay employees. Any commissions represent an addition to payment, but because commissions cannot be guaranteed they cannot compensate for lower minimum wage.

11. D: The phrase adverse impact or unintentional discrimination refers to the selection rate of a protected class being less than 80% of the selection rate of the highest group. In other words, if the selection rate of females is less than 80% the selection rate of males, there is an adverse impact on females by the hiring process. Answer choice A is the opposite of the correct definition of adverse

impact, so it is incorrect. Answer choice B is close to the meaning of adverse impact – in a broad sense – but it is not specific enough to be correct. Answer choice C is also too broad, particularly because there is far more to the Uniform Guidelines on Employee Selection Process than just selection rate. And answer choice E is incorrect; while adverse impact might be interpreted as discrimination, it is not necessarily the direct result of discrimination.

12. C: While a consideration of the economic situation might be useful, it is not a part of the human resources professional's analysis of staffing needs. The other answer choices – creating a list of necessary KSAs that will encourage company growth, developing a list of employees who might be ready for promotion, considering hiring options for open positions, and reviewing the results of hiring decisions for future hiring – are all part of an analysis of staffing needs.

13. A: For applications that are completed in-house – that is, for internal applications that current employees complete – a short-form application is usually best. This is because the company will already have most of the employee's information on file and simply needs a formal application for the new job rather than an extensive application detailing information the company probably has. Answer choice B is incorrect because the weighted employment application, while specific to the job and excellent for considering the details of a candidate's qualifications, is far too costly to establish in this type of situation. Answer choice C is incorrect because the long-form application is simply unnecessary for internal hiring. Answer choice D is incorrect because the job-specific application (which is used largely for hiring a number of employees for similar positions) will not necessarily be useful for the company looking to hire internally. And answer choice E is incorrect because an application is almost always necessary, even for internal hiring.

14. A: When a department within a company is planning interviews to hire new employees, the human resources professional's role is primarily one of assisting. The human resources professional is not responsible for choosing the members of the prospective interview board (answer choice B), since this role will fall to the department and those who will be working with the new employee or employees. Additionally, the job of creating official list of questions for the interview (answer choice C), conducting the actual interviews for prospective employees (answer choice D), and working with the interview board to select the right candidate (answer choice E) belongs not to the human resources professional but to the manager or supervisor of department in which the employees will work.

15. B: Specific questions regarding a candidate's personal life and religious choices are entirely off limits for interviews. The only question that an interviewer may ask a candidate is whether or not the candidate belongs to an organization that may be relevant to the job. Unless the candidate volunteers information, all other questions about the religious symbol that the candidate is wearing are not appropriate during the interview. This is because a question could make a candidate uncomfortable. What is more, should the candidate be asked such a question and then receive the job – or not receive the job – the situation could be viewed as a form of discrimination.

16. C: Caspar's interview bias is one of contrast; he finds himself, however unconsciously, contrasting the other candidates with the first candidate that he interviews. A cultural noise bias (answer choice A) occurs when the candidate responds with pointed answers that are aimed at making the interviewer happy rather than responding in a more natural or general way. A halo bias (answer choice B) occurs when the interviewer considers only one quality of the candidate over his other qualities, such as shyness that might detract from the candidate's true record of achievement. A leniency bias (answer choice D) means the interviewer is lenient in regard to a candidate's

potential weaknesses. A negative emphasis bias (answer choice E) means the interviewer places too much weight on the candidate's weaknesses.

17. E: Louisa's response to the candidate is influenced by her first impression of the candidate's behavior. A knowledge-of-predictor bias (answer choice A) means the interviewer responds to the candidate based on knowledge about the candidate's scores on evaluative tests that were given. A stereotyping bias (answer choice B) occurs when an interviewer bases a personal opinion about a candidate on a stereotype of the candidate rather than evaluating the candidate as objectively as possible. A recency bias (answer choice C) means the interviewer compares a candidate to the most recent candidate that was interviewed. A nonverbal bias occurs when the interviewer is over-influenced by body language instead of by the candidate's responses.

18. D: The Uniform Guidelines on Employee Selection Process (UGESP) requires that all testing be focused around reliability and validity. Answer choice A is incorrect, not because "fairness" is an undesirable quality but because it is intended to be a result of the requirements of validity and reliability. Answer choice B is also incorrect because "disinterestedness" is an intended result of the required qualities of reliability and validity. Answer choice C is incorrect, again because "equality" is an expected result, and answer choice D is incorrect because "consideration" is too vague of a requirement for establishing tests.

19. B: The required qualities of reliability and validity are established for the express purpose of avoiding discrimination against protected classes. Answer choice A is incorrect because it makes no sense to ensure the same results from all tests – the tests would have no value at that point. Answer choice C is incorrect because the testing of candidates for a new position is about assessing the qualifications of the candidates and not quantifying the success rate of the company. Answer choice D is incorrect because it is too vague. Such guidelines would always be intended to create better standards for testing, but this is not specific enough to be a correct answer. And answer choice E is correct in the larger sense but is also not specific enough, since the standards were created for very specific reasons.

20. E: The WARN Act is the Worker Adjustment and Retraining Notification Act, which was designed to offer rights for workers who have been laid off. Answer choice A is incorrect because the act was certainly not designed to prevent massive lay-offs but rather to give workers "adjustment and retraining" in the event of massive lay-offs. Answer choice B is incorrect because the act cannot necessarily provide new positions for workers who have been laid off. Answer choice C is incorrect; while the act creates government funding for workers who have lost their jobs, it does not create government funding for a struggling company. And answer choice D is incorrect because the act cannot provide severance pay for those who have been laid off.

21. E: Organization development is the process by which a human resources professional analyzes the elements of an organization's makeup and considers opportunities for improvement. Answer choice A is incorrect because the definition refers more to organization culture than it does to organization development. And answer choices B, C, and D are incorrect because they refer to elements of organization development but do not explain the larger definition of the process as a whole.

22. C: The four categories of intervention, as presented by Cummings and Worley in Organization Development and Change, are Techno-structural, Human Resource Management, Human Process, and Strategic. Change management is more of another way to describe intervention within an organization than it is a category of intervention.

23. D: In the workplace, the Meyers-Brigg Type Indicator is primarily used as a personality test to enable individuals to understand their personalities better and to assist staff members in appreciating how to interact with their co-workers more effectively. Due to the nature of the administrative department and its situation – employees who work together quite frequently and run into personality conflicts – the Meyers-Brigg test will be Raisa's best recommendation. Answer choices A and C are incorrect because research has suggested a lack of long-term value in team-building activities such as obstacle courses and scavenger hunts. Answer choices B and E are also incorrect: while role-playing situations and real-life scenarios might be beneficial to those who work in highly active and often sensitive fields, they will not necessarily be as useful for employees whose jobs is more focused around completing and maintaining paperwork for a university.

24. A: The instructional design acronym known as the ADDIE model begins not with Administration but with Analysis. The other options – Design, Development, Implementation, and Evaluation – are all accurate elements of the ADDIE acronym.

25. B: Facilitation is an instructional method that enables employees to work together on problem-solving techniques while under the guidance of a facilitator, or third-party expert in helping different groups interact effectively. Answer choice A is incorrect because the vestibule instructional method is a type of simulation, in which the employees receive hands-on experience on the equipment they will be using. A demonstration is largely just a presentation of information in a lecture-style setting, so that would be inappropriate for this situation, making answer choice C incorrect. Similarly, a conference style of instructional method is primarily focused on presenting information without employee interaction, so answer choice D is also incorrect. And the one-on-one method would be instruction given from one person to another. This is hardly useful in the situation with which Eamon is presented, so answer choice E is incorrect.

26. D: The purpose of a total rewards strategy is one of reviewing the budget and finding out how much of the budget is available for establishing rewards that will retain employees. (Additionally, the total rewards strategy contributes to drawing potential employees and motivating them in their employment activities.) Answer choice A is incorrect. While a total rewards program might cover salaries, the total rewards strategy is larger than basic salary. Answer choice B is incorrect because the total rewards strategy is unrelated to employer brand. Answer choice C is incorrect because the total rewards strategy is unconnected to creating teamwork among employees. And answer choice E is incorrect because the total rewards strategy is unrelated to the recognition of organizational changes.

27. B: When establishing employee compensation within an organization, considering employee salary history might be a part of the larger process, but it is not a major factor in the process. Answer choices A, C, D, and E – IRS rules, conditions in the labor market, current economic situations, and competition from other companies – all play a major role in establishing employee compensation.

28. E: The McNamara-O'Hara Service Contract Act (1965) covers federal service contracts, but the Fair Labor Standards Act does not. The Fair Labor Standards Act does, however, cover minimum wage requirements, exemption conditions for employees, work conditions for children under 18, and overtime. As a result, answer choices A, B, C, and D are all incorrect.

29. A: Benchmark positions are simply the types of positions that are common within all organizations, such as administrative assistants. Benchmark positions do not, however, relate to an evaluation of current jobs (answer choice B), a review of market conditions for salaries (answer

- 128 -

choice C), a change in significant jobs in a company (answer choice D), and a review of the value of various positions within an organization (answer choice E).

30. C: According to FMLA guidelines, an employee must work for an employer for a minimum of 12 months (not necessarily consecutively) in order to apply for FMLA-approved leave. Because Arthur has only worked for the company for 9 months, he will not be eligible to apply for type of leave, which is what Brad – as the human resources professional – will be required to explain to Arthur. Answer choices A, B, D, and E are incorrect because each represents the wrong period of time for FMLA leave.

31. B: COBRA regulations state that a company with at least 20 employees must provide a defined amount of health benefits for employees. Answer choices A, C, D, and E are all correct because they fail to recognize the requirements of COBRA regarding minimum number of employees.

32. A: Among the answer choices provided, only the Family Medical and Leave Act does not reference or cover employee deferred compensation programs. The Retirement Equity Act (answer choice B), the Small Business Job Protection Act (answer choice C), the Older Worker Benefit Protection Act (answer choice D), and the Pension Protection Act (answer choice E) all provide for deferred employee compensation programs in some way.

33. D: The Health Insurance Portability and Accountability Act was added to ERISA for the express purpose of forbidding any type of health benefit discrimination toward employees based on pre-existing health problems or health conditions. Answer choice A is incorrect for several reasons. On the one hand, it is simply too vague to explain the purpose of HIPAA. What is more, answer choice A does not simply establish new guidelines for employee health insurance programs, so it is incorrect. Answer choices B and C are incorrect because both refer to COBRA (answer choice B references COBRA inferentially), and HIPAA is not immediately connected to COBRA or to providing minimum health benefits for employees. Answer choice E is incorrect because it fails to specify the exact purpose of HIPAA and because HIPAA was not added to ERISA simply for the purpose of retired employees maintaining healthcare coverage.

34. D: Question 34 describes the defined benefit program, which starts with a basic pension plan. To this pension plan are added established benefits, thus explaining the name of the plan. Answer choice A is incorrect because the benefit accrual plan is not a type of voluntary benefits plan. Answer choice B is incorrect. Like the defined benefit plan, the defined contribution plan utilizes a standard pension plan but without the added benefits defined in advance. Answer choice C is incorrect because the nonqualified plan provides benefits to specified employees (for example, executives) and shareholders. And answer choice E is incorrect because a qualified plan is a 401(k) plan that receives special tax credits from the IRS.

35. B: Question 35 describes the nonqualified plan, which provides benefits to employees such as executives and shareholders. Answer choice A is incorrect because the qualified plan provides IRS-approved tax advantages but without any extra benefits for shareholders and executives. Answer choice C is incorrect because the defined contribution plan utilizes a standard pension plan without any added benefits defined in advance. Answer choice D is incorrect because the defined benefit program starts with a pension plan and adds specified benefits to it. Answer choice E is incorrect because participation benefit is not a type of voluntary benefits plan.

36. A: The Glass Ceiling Act noted that the three barriers to women advancing in the workplace are internal, societal, and governmental. Answer choices B and D are incorrect because the term

- 129 -

"federal" encompasses government at the federal level but does not include any local or state governmental barriers that might exist for women in the workplace. Answer choices C and E are incorrect because an economic barrier would be a result of other barriers or would fall under "societal" barriers.

37. D: The Latin phrase quid pro quo translates simply as this for that and under sexual harassment laws it suggests that an employee is expected to provide sexual favors for improved (or continued) employment situation. Answer choices A, B, C, and E are incorrect because they do not reflect a correct translation of this Latin phrase.

38. E: The rights that are provided by the NLRA apply to all employees of an organization and are not limited to specific employees within that organization. As a result, the other answer choices that limit the employee coverage to full-time employees only (answer choice A), part-time employees only (answer choice B), union employees only (answer choice C), and non-union employees only (answer choice D) are all incorrect.

39. B: Featherbedding occurs when a union requires that an otherwise obsolete job remains intact at an organization in order to avoid terminating an employee. Answer choice A is incorrect because it describes a hot cargo agreement. Answer choice C is incorrect because it simply describes a type of union coercion. Answer choice D is incorrect because it describes another type of union coercion or restraint of employees. And answer choice E is incorrect because it describes a type of employer coercion or restraint, but it does not describe featherbedding.

40. D: When an employer discovers that employees are beginning to unionize, the employer is not allowed to prevent unionization. The employer can, however, provide information to employees about the problems involved with unionization. Answer choice A is incorrect because the employer may not contact union leaders and forbid unionization. Answer choice B is incorrect because employers are not allowed to block employees who begin to unionize. Answer choice C is incorrect because employers may not threaten to replace workers who choose to unionize (although employers may replace workers during a lawful economic strike). Answer choice E is incorrect because employers are allowed to discuss unionization with employees; however, the substance of that discussion can be restricted by law.

41. E: The category of labor relations is not considered to be one of the larger risks that a human resources professional must consider. Compliance with labor relations laws would fall under the category of legal compliance as a whole, but it is not a separate area of risk management. Answer choices A, B, C, and E are all incorrect because they represent distinct areas of risk that a human resources professional must consider.

42. C: The purpose of a human resources audit can be fairly extensive in scope--to consider overall improvements that can be made within the company. Answer choice A is incorrect because a human resources audit is certainly not limited to the human resources department, nor would a review of the organization within the human resources department represent an audit. Answer choice B is incorrect because it is too limited in focus. A human resources audit might include a review of compliance with labor relations laws, but it is not the only focus of a human resources audit. Answer choices D and E are also incorrect because they are do not include the larger purpose of the human resources audit and focus only on elements of the audit.

43. B: The Drug-Free Workplace Act of 1988 applies specifically to federal contractors (specifically, the contractors that make at least $100,000). Answer choices A, C, D, and E are incorrect because

they inaccurately reflect the types of organizations to which the Drug-Free Workplace Act of 1988 refers. Specifically, answer choice A is incorrect because it is far too vague. A federal contractor might be a large corporation, but not all large corporations are going to be federal contractors. Answer choice C is incorrect because federal contractors might be funded through government agencies but are entirely different organizations. Answer choice D is incorrect because it simply makes no sense: all local businesses will, in some way, be governed under municipal laws. Answer choice E is also incorrect because academic organizations – like most business that are not federal contractors – are responsible for developing their own substance abuse policies for the workplace.

44. A: The piece of legislation to which the quote refers is the Occupational Safety and Health Act of 1970 (OSHA). The Americans with Disabilities Act (ADA) is focused specifically on providing rights for employees with disabilities in the workplace. The Drug-Free Workplace Act is focused on the substance abuse policy for federal contractors. The Sarbanes-Oxley Act is focused on the legal obligation that organizations have to record and report financial information. And the Fair Labor Standards Act refers to the legal requirements that companies have to provide a workplace environment that is fair to all employees.

45. C: The stated categories of OSHA violations include willful, serious, other-than-serious, repeat, failure to abate, and de minimus (or minimal violations). Accidental is not one of the categories officially noted by OSHA, so answer choice C is correct. Answer choices A, B, D, and E all reflect actual categories, so they are incorrect.

46. B: Organizations with up to 10 employees are not required to file OSHA forms. As a result, organizations with a minimum of 11 employees must file OSHA forms. Answer choices A, C, D, and E are incorrect because they reflect the incorrect number of employees for filing OSHA documentation.

47. E: The purpose of the Needlestick Safety and Prevention Act is to require the employers report workplace injuries as a result of sharp objects and consider replacement objects to prevent further injuries. Answer choice A is incorrect because the purpose of the act is not to require that companies perform quarterly audits. Answer choice B is incorrect because the Needlestick Safety and Prevention Act does not require that organizations remove specified sharp objects but instead recommend the replacement of dangerous sharp objects. Answer choice C is incorrect because the act does not create a list of sharp objects that are recognized for having caused workplace injuries but instead leaves the decision about these objects up to the organization. Answer choice D is incorrect because the act does not require that companies pay a fine for workplace injuries from sharp objects.

48. D: The human resources professional is not required to provide for all employee accommodation requests to ensure continued employment. Human resources professionals are expected to discuss possible employee accommodations with management and to recommend the implementation of certain requests, but there is no requirement to implement all requests. Answer choices A, B, C, and E are all steps in the human resources professional's role in observing the guidelines of ADA, so they are incorrect.

49. B: The three primary types of plans that OSHA requires organizations to develop include an injury and illness prevention plan, an emergency response plan, and a fire prevention plan. Answer choice A is incorrect because OSHA does not require a drug prevention plan. Such a plan might fall under illness prevention, but ultimately a drug prevention plan is voluntary on the part of the organization. Answer choice C is incorrect because OSHA does not require an environmental

- 131 -

protection plan. This too might fall under illness prevention, but it is not specified under OSHA's rules. Answer choice D is incorrect because OSHA does not require a clean air plan. Additionally, answer choice E is incorrect because OSHA does not require that organizations create a terrorism response plan.

50. A: However organizations choose to create their plans, a company policy about employee protection is required for all of them. This policy lets employees know what the organization's approach to employee protection is. Answer choice B is incorrect because a disaster recovery plan is not a necessary part of the three plans. Answer choice C is incorrect because organizations are not obligated to include hazard assessment in all three plans. Answer choice D is incorrect because organizations are not required to include a union policy about employee protection. And answer choice E is incorrect because organizations are not required to create a fellow servant rule. In fact, the fellow servant rule is a part of common law doctrine that is now considered obsolete.

51. C: A due diligence process during a merger should focus primarily on recording the following basics of company employee details: documentation regarding employee names, employment contracts, I-9 forms, benefit contracts, compensation information, company policy and procedures (such as handbooks for employees), compliance documentation for equal opportunity, information about company labor relations (including labor activity), all information about potential legal situations (such as legal violations, sexual harassment claims, and disputes about employee terminations), and legal compliance documentation for COBRA, FMLA, WARN, and OSHA. This means that answer choices A, B, D, and E all fall within the boundaries of due diligence for a merger, leaving only answer choice C. What is more, whistleblower prevention is not necessarily legal – as there are a number of laws designed to protect whistleblowers – so a company could not legally retain or utilize whistleblower techniques.

52. B: In many cases, the human resources professional is responsible for acting as a kind of median between the company and its employees. In organizations, the role of the human resources professional is somewhat more specific; the HR professional is expected to encourage employees in their strengths and when necessary, help employees in building their strengths. Answer choice A is incorrect. While the HR professional's responsibility is related to change in organizations, it cannot produce definitive change if the need is too great. Answer choice C can be correct in the greater sense of the HR professional's job, but is not specific enough for the HR professional's responsibility within organizations. Similarly, answer choices D and E relate to the HR professional's job description but not within organizations.

53. B: The steps for Enterprise Risk Management are focused primarily on identifying risk and pursuing means of managing and reducing risk. As a result, this includes answer choices A, C, D, and E. The steps of Enterprise Risk Management do not, however, include identifying the employees who are responsible for the risk. This might be part of the larger process of understanding risk, but it does not fall under the primary steps of Enterprise Risk Management. Answer choice B is, therefore, correct.

54. D: According to the expectations of ERM, a human resources professional should apply reasonable techniques to correcting a problem. In Harold's case, the best option for addressing the problem of the incomplete documentation would simply be to establish a quarterly review of the paperwork to ensure that it is completed. As for the other answer choices, they each contain extreme responses that do not fit with the requirements of ERM. Terminating the responsible employee does not guarantee that the problem will be fully addressed. Creating a new department simply adds more paper work that can further complicate the process of completing the

documentation. There is nothing within the process of ERM that suggests a human resources professional can request a reprieve from a federal agency; the rules are in place already and need to be observed. And while creating a series of checklists sounds good, it also sounds vague and has the potential to be as ineffective as the current system.

55. A: A reduced number of lawsuits against a company definitely indicates that the human resources department is bringing value to a company. Lawsuits often occur when serious policy mistakes are made. If policy mistakes are being reduced or eliminated, the company is moving in a positive direction. Answer choice B is incorrect because an increase in expenses within the human resources department indicates nothing more in the immediate sense than that the human resource department is spending more money. Whether or not that money is being put to good use is not explained sufficiently. Answer choice C makes no sense because an increase in employee complaints cannot indicate if any department – and definitely not the human resources department – is bringing value to the company. Similar to answer choice A, answer choice D does not show anything tangible in terms of value; an increase in employees within human resources only shows that more people are needed and not that better work is being done. And answer choice E has no real relevance to human resources. Outsourcing occurs for a variety of reasons that may or may not relate to the value that the human resources department brings to a company.

56. A: The Herzberg Motivation/Hygiene Theory, developed by Frederick Herzberg in 1959, was the result of Herzberg's study on what motivated employees and the way that positive motivation could bring quantifiable results to a company. Herzberg concluded that giving employees the opportunity to excel in something will bring overall success to the entire company.

57. C: The McGregor X and Y Theory broke management up into two different styles, called X and Y for the study. McGregor concluded that the X-style manager is focused more on close supervision and control of employees, while the Y-style manager seeks to create a rewarding work environment for all employees. McGregor's theory is based on Maslow Hierarchy Theory, but it achieves separate conclusions, so answer choice A is not correct.

58. B: B.F. Skinner is famous as a behaviorist, concluding that all human actions can be conditioned through behavior modification, or different types of behavioral reinforcement.

59. E: The Genetic Information Nondiscrimination Act of 2008 does not make employers responsible for information acquired by accident. With that information, however, employers have no legal right to make decisions or change an employee's work situation, so Abbey's only option is to keep the information to herself and take no action. Answer choice A is incorrect because the law does not require Abbey to report the employee's personal information to her superiors, nor should she take such a step. Answer choice B is incorrect because the Department of Labor does not need to be updated on this type of individual employee information (and reporting it could make Abbey legally responsible for divulging an employee's personal details). Answer choice C is incorrect because Abbey has no legal responsibility to discuss the situation with the employee, nor should she counsel the employee about changing the work situation. Answer choice D is also incorrect because employee genetic information – if obtained by accident – should not be documented. In fact, documenting it could create legal problems for the company, so Abbey's only choice is to proceed as though she does not know the information.

60. A: Marcus Buckingham and Curt Coffman's First, Break All the Rules takes a positive approach to improving the situation for employees; terminating an employee would not necessarily create a positive situation. Instead, Buckingham and Coffman suggest that a human resources professional

work on the steps provided in answer choices B, C, D, and E, which are creating goals, focusing on individual employee strengths, identifying employee KSAs, and locating the most advantageous work situation for employees.

61. B: The Training Adjustment Assistance (TAA) program was designed specifically to provide assistance to employees who have lost their jobs due to a rise in the number of imports. In other words, when import levels shift and companies in the US begin importing items that were previously manufactured here, the manufacturing companies might close as a result leaving employees without jobs. Answer choice A is incorrect because the TAA was designed for a far more particular reason than just employees losing their jobs for any reason. Answer choice C is incorrect because the TAA is related to providing training for laid-off workers to receive new jobs instead of providing them with health benefits. Answer choice D is incorrect because the TAA program is designed for workers who have already lost their jobs rather than for those who currently have jobs. Answer choice E is incorrect because the TAA does not specifically work with welfare, while the Workforce Investment Act (WIA) does.

62. E: The process described in question 12 is that of recruiting, or making the details of making the position available to interested candidates and pursuing potential employees who will fill the requirements of the job as best as possible. Answer choice A is incorrect because the process of hiring follows the process of recruiting. Answer choice B is incorrect because the process of sourcing is related more to acquiring the names and other information of potential candidates but is considered separate from recruiting. Answer choice C is incorrect because tracking is also a separate process from recruiting. Answer choice D is incorrect because selection is the next step beyond recruiting but does not belong within the recruitment process.

63. B: The process of succession planning requires that a human resources professional consider employees within their current positions. As a result, answer choice B falls outside the focus on employees within the positions and instead focuses on the position itself. This is not a part of succession planning. Answer choices A, C, D, and E all belong to the process of categorizing employees who are currently in positions within an organization.

64. C: By allowing his intuition to guide his preference, Eric is relying on the bias of his gut feeling. Answer choice A is incorrect because a first impression bias means the interviewer allows an immediate impression of a candidate to determine a decision. Answer choice B is incorrect because a cultural noise bias means the candidate responds with pointed answers that are aimed at making the interviewer happy rather than responding in a more natural or general way. Answer choice D is incorrect because a leniency bias is occurs when the interviewer is lenient in regard to a candidate and fails to take potential weaknesses into account. Answer choice E is incorrect because a nonverbal bias occurs when the interviewer is over-influenced by body language instead of by the candidate's responses.

65. A: In this case, Jocelyn is allowing a stereotyping bias (how she perceives a female mechanic) to guide her decision about which candidate will be best for the position in the auto repair shop. Answer choice B is incorrect because a similar-to-me bias occurs when the interviewer is influenced by similar interests or a similar background in the candidate. Answer choice C is incorrect because a recency bias occurs when the interviewer compares a candidate to the previously interviewed candidate. Answer choice D is incorrect because a first impression bias happens when an immediate impression of a candidate determines a decision. And answer choice E is incorrect because a gut feeling bias relies on a preference or intuition to make a decision about a candidate.

66. C: An employer brand is simply a clear indication of a company's identity; it is essentially the unique characteristic(s) that define a company. An employer brand might be related to a public relations strategy (answer choice A), but it is not contained entirely within the public relations strategy. Similarly, the human resources policy of marketing (answer choice B) might reflect the employer brand, but this is not a clear definition of it. The total rewards philosophy is a separate part of a company's identity, so answer choice D is incorrect. And while the company might design a logo that reflects its employer brand, the logo is not equivalent to the brand.

67. A: Because the new employees will be working with the heads of several departments, the panel interview style is best. It enables each of the department heads to be there during the interview process. A behavioral interview might be useful in some cases, but there is nothing specific about this case that would require candidates to indicate how their prior behavior would affect the current position. A patterned interview might be useful, but it will not necessarily be the most useful type of interview for this situation. A stress interview is unnecessary for this type of position (database management). Finally, a nondirective interview has no clear value for the type of position being filled.

68. A: Simply put, the conditions in the labor market can influence the available candidates for open positions in a company. Answer choice B might be correct in the larger, but conditions in the labor market do not have to have a negative effect on the bottom line. An analysis of competition with other companies might result from overall economic changes, but changes in the labor market do not necessarily cause this, so answer choice C is incorrect. Answer choice D might also be accurate in a broad way, but this is not clear enough for an immediate connection to the changes in the labor market and the way that they affect a company. Answer choice E contains interesting information, but it is not relevant to the way that changes in the labor market affect a company.

69. D: The Foreign Corrupt Practices Act (FCPA) was created specifically to prevent American businesses from bribing foreign governments. This act has nothing to do with the illegal trafficking of merchandise (answer choice A) or changing the level of imports (answer choice B). And while the larger role of the act is to maintain fair standards, answer choice C is incorrect because it is not clear about the nature of these fair standards. And answer choice E is incorrect because the FCPA is not relevant to protecting American workers overseas but rather focuses on the relationship between American businesses and foreign governments.

70. E: Polygraph tests are allowed among federal defense contractors but may only be administered to those who will be working in the defense-related jobs. Most large contractors will not limit their contract work to the government, so it is entirely possible that the company will have employees doing work that is unrelated to the defense jobs. What is more, the employees who do work in connection with the defense agency but do not necessarily do sensitive work will not require polygraph testing. As a result, answer choice A is incorrect because there is no justification for testing all employees of the contractor. Answer choice B is incorrect because federal law does allow for polygraph testing in certain situations. Answer choice C is incorrect because it does not really address the question and because the information is not accurate--polygraph tests must be administered by certified professionals. Answer choice D is also incorrect because the nature of the contractor's work for the defense agency will likely justify polygraph testing for many of the employees.

71. A: The purpose of talent management is twofold: to create a reputation and working situation that draws in new talent and to hold on to the talent by constantly maintaining the most effective work situation for employees. Answer choice A best summarizes this description, so it is correct.

Answer choices B, D, and E all contain descriptions that are part of talent management, but each fails to encompass the entire purpose of talent management. As a result, answer choices B, D, and E are all incorrect. Answer choice C is also incorrect because it steps beyond any purpose of talent management. The goal of this process is not to train all employees for promotion but rather to attract employees with significant talent and to maintain them within the organization.

72. D: The development of new and more effective training material might be an end result of training analysis, but it is not necessarily one of the primary steps within the process. Answer choices A, B, C, and E, however, all reflect specific steps within the process of analyzing training and are thus incorrect.

73. B: As the question states, the training will encompass several features – lectures, film presentations, and group work. Among the available styles of seating, the chevron-style – with the chairs angled in a V-shape toward the stage or front of the meeting space – will offer the most versatility for trainees. Answer choice A is incorrect because the theater-style seating would be useful for lectures and film presentations but would offer no good way for trainees to break into groups. Answer choice C is incorrect because the banquet-style seating would be excellent for group work but would be impractical for lectures and film presentations. Similarly, answer choice D is incorrect because the conference-style seating would place participants around one large table, which would not necessarily be useful for any of the three activities that will occur in the training. And answer choice E is incorrect because the U-shaped seating would be useful only for lectures but would not benefit the trainees in a film presentation or in group work.

74. E: Question 24 describes a results-based evaluation--an evaluation in which a goal or objective is noted in advance and then reviewed after a stated period of time. Answer choice A is incorrect because a reaction-style evaluation usually consists of a survey of some kind, which does not apply to the situation described in the question. Answer choice B is also incorrect because the learning-style evaluation focuses on whether or not employees actually learned required information correctly instead of whether or not a stated objective was reached. Answer choice C is a subset of answer choice B (the pre-test / posttest of the learning-style evaluation), so it is incorrect. Answer choice D is incorrect because the behavior-style evaluation takes a broader look at an employee's work and accomplishments instead of focusing on a stated goal and evaluating whether or not it was reached.

75. C: The responsibility of the human resources professional in is to recognize that employees need a balance of work and situation outside of work in order to be the most effective in the workplace. Answer choices A, B, D, and E all contain aspects of considering unique employee needs – in particular, with the focus on diversity initiatives, flexibility in work situation, and repatriation – but only answer choice C encompasses all of the HR responsibility.

76. C: The primary role of fiduciary responsibility for the human resources professional is to handle the total rewards program for an organization. Answer choices A, B, D, and E are incorrect, not because they are unrelated to fiduciary responsibility, but because they do not represent the primary role of fiduciary responsibility for a human resources professional. While handling a total rewards program, the human resources professional is expected to create unimpeachable trust, avoid any indication of favoritism, recognize the need for handle sensitive material carefully, and assure a sense of trust in the organization's total rewards program.

77. B: Each company is responsible for establishing the vacation pay policies that will apply to the employees of that company. The FMLA does not specify vacation pay policies, so answer choice A is

- 136 -

incorrect. ERISA is the Employee Retirement Income Security Act of 1974, so it does not relate to vacation pay policies; therefore, answer choice C is incorrect. States do not establish vacation pay guidelines (apart from basic compensation requirements established at the federal level), so answer choice D is incorrect. And unions might vote for changes within vacation pay policies, but they are not responsible for creating these policies, so answer choice E is incorrect.

78. A: Workers compensation laws state that employers are responsible for any work-related injuries or problems that employees sustain on the job. Answer choice B is incorrect because employers are not responsible for all or any of an individual's health problems unless of course they were sustained at work. Answer choice C is incorrect because the workers compensation laws do not necessarily place the full burden of proof on employees to prove the nature of the injury or problem. Answer choice D is incorrect because the workers compensation laws do not provide for federal aid. Answer choice E is incorrect because there is no federally designated list of injuries for which employers are responsible.

79. D: Cash-balance plans fall under the category of deferred contribution but not under the category of defined contribution. Answer choices A, B, C, and E – 401(k), money purchase plans, profit-sharing plans, and target benefit plans – do, however, fall under defined contribution from employers toward employee retirement accounts.

80. A: The "golden" benefits for executive compensation packages include the golden parachute (answer choice B), the golden handshake (answer choice C), the golden handcuffs (answer choice D), and the golden life jacket (answer choice E). There is no golden lifeboat, however, so answer choice A is correct because it does not fall within this category of benefits for executive compensation packages.

81. B: The fiduciary role of the human resources professional regarding ERISA is primarily one of handling and managing the pension funds that the organization provides for retirement accounts. Answer choice A is incorrect because the fiduciary role does not include setting up pension accounts for employees. (This might be another part of the human resources professional's job, but this is not the immediate fiduciary role with respect to ERISA.) Answer choice C is incorrect because the fiduciary role has nothing to do with ensuring that HIPAA guidelines are observed. Answer choice D is incorrect because human resources professional is not responsible for creating retirement account rules. And answer choice E is incorrect because the fiduciary role of the human resources professional is not necessarily one of locating the funding but rather of managing it.

82. C: Once a company has filed ERISA records with the Department of Labor, that company is required to maintain those records for a minimum of six years. Answer choices A, B, D, and E are incorrect because they do not reflect accurate federal guidelines for ERISA record keeping.

83. E: The Personal Responsibility and Work Opportunity Reconciliation Act, which went into law in 1996, establishes and updates rules for retaining and reporting employee identification records. Answer choice A is incorrect because the Fair Labor Standards Act has no immediate requirement about record keeping and instead focuses on establishing fair compensation for employees. Answer choice B is incorrect because the Fair Credit Reporting Act governs employee credit reporting but not the retention of employee identification records. Answer choice C is incorrect because the workplace application of the Consumer Credit Protection Act relates to wage garnishing. And answer choice D is incorrect because the Small Business Job Protection Act relates to employee deferred compensation plans.

84. C: Question 34 describes the qualified plan, which provides IRS-approved tax advantages but without any extra benefits for shareholders and executives. Answer choice A is incorrect because the nonqualified plan provides benefits to specified employees (i.e., executives) and shareholder. Answer choice B is incorrect because the defined contribution plan utilizes a standard pension plan but without the added benefits defined in advance. Answer choice D is incorrect because the cash balance plan is a combination of the defined benefit and defined contribution plan but does not fall under the immediate grouping of voluntary benefits programs. Answer choice E is incorrect because the defined benefit program starts with a pension plan and adds specified benefits to it.

85. E: Question 35 describes the defined contribution plan, which utilizes a standard pension plan but without the added benefits defined in advance. Answer choice A is incorrect because participation benefits do not refer to a voluntary benefits program. Answer choice B is incorrect because the nonqualified plan provides benefits to specified employees (i.e., executives) and shareholder. Answer choice C is incorrect because the cash balance plan is a combination of the defined benefit and defined contribution plan but does not fall under the immediate grouping of voluntary benefits programs. And answer choice D is incorrect because it provides IRS-approved tax advantages but without any extra benefits for shareholders and executives.

86. A: Though picketing is legal under certain circumstances, one instance when picketing is illegal occurs when an election for union representation has occurred within a 12-month period. Answer choices B, C, D, and E are all incorrect because they represent occasions when picketing would be considered legal.

87. B: Principled bargaining is considered a collective bargaining position, but it is not considered a collective bargaining strategy. Answer choices, A, C, D, and E are all incorrect because they represent four types of collective bargaining strategies.

88. E: While some types of strikes are fully legal, a sit-down strike is considered illegal. Double breasting is a reference to different types of businesses-- one being union and the other being non-union--and it has no immediate connection to bargaining strategies, so answer choice A is incorrect. A lockout is the result of an employer stopping work indefinitely, but it is not a bargaining strategy, so answer choice B is incorrect. A secondary boycott is the result of a union attempting to require the participation of a secondary employer who is not directly involved in a union issue with the primary employer, so answer choice C is incorrect. Common situs picketing is the result of two employers sharing a business location when one of the employers is engaged in a labor dispute with employees, so answer choice D is incorrect.

89. C: An unfair labor practice is defined as any activity from an employer or a union that hinders employees from exercising their rights. Answer choices A, B, D, and E are incorrect. While they describe types of unfair labor practices, they fail to provide a complete definition of ULP. Each offers a type of unfair labor practice, but does not encompass the total definition.

90. B: During a lawful economic strike, employers do have the right to hire employees to replace the striking employees. Answer choices A, C, D, and E are incorrect because they each represent types of unfair labor practices. Employers may not fire employees who refuse to cease striking instead of returning to work. They also may not encourage the union to disband and/or suggest the formation of a new union. Nor may the employer disband union bargaining and require new representation, or restrict union bargaining if this negatively impacts company's finances.

91. D: OSHA does not list computer use as one of its standard environmental health hazards. Computer use might contribute to other hazards (such as ergonomic design or stress), but it is not in itself a health hazard. Answer choices A, B, C, and E are incorrect because each represents one of OSHA's environmental health hazards.

92. C: Employers are legally allowed to check and review employee email as long as they provide a written policy informing employees of the potential for email searches. Without this written policy, employers could legally file concerns about invasion of employee privacy. Answer choice A is incorrect because immediate notification from the legal department of impending review would not be sufficient. Answer choice B is incorrect because evidence of employee wrongdoing is too late for an employer to implement a search policy. Answer choice D is incorrect because notification is required. Although employers technically own the emails that employees send and receive, they are not advised to search emails without a written search policy. Answer choice E is incorrect because employers are allowed to check and review employee emails.

93. E: According to NIOSH, this is the definition of stress that affects employees in the workplace. Answer choice A is incorrect because it should be considered an effect of stress but does not fulfill the requirements of the definition. Answer choice B, C, and D are incorrect because they too could be considered by-products of stress but do not reflect the definition provided by NIOSH.

94. A: If an employee is accused of inappropriate behavior toward other employees, the company management has an obligation to conduct a workplace investigation. Answer choice B is incorrect because a workplace investigation is related to activities and behavior in the workplace; a rapid reduction in the price of the stock would not require a workplace investigation. Answer choice C is incorrect because company management would not require a workplace investigation due to a breach in legal compliance. Answer choice D is incorrect because disagreements among co-workers are par for the course in the workplace. It is the substance of the disagreement that might cause a workplace investigation. Answer choice E is incorrect because management would not require a workplace investigation due to organizational problems within the human resources department.

95. A: The EEOC, or the Equal Employment Opportunity Commission, is responsible for risk management activities that cover Civil Rights. The SOX (The Sarbanes-Oxley Act) covers a company's obligation to report financial matters. OSHA (the Occupational Safety and Health Act) covers safety and health in the workplace. The SEC (Securities and Exchange Commission) covers workplace security – and primarily financial security. And the MSHA (Mine Safety and Health Administration) covers mine safety for workers in different types of mines.

96. D: The unholy trinity refers to the common law doctrines of the fellow servant rule, the doctrine of contributory negligence, and the voluntary assumption of risk that traditionally reflected worker's compensation guidelines in the U.S. Answer choices A, B, C, and E are incorrect because they fail to provide the accurate items contained within the phrase unholy trinity.

97. C: OSHA 300 is officially the Log of Work-Related Injuries and Illnesses. Answer choice A is incorrect because it more closely reflects OSHA 300A, which is a separate log. Answer choice B is incorrect because the Injury and Illness Incident Report is officially OSHA 301. Answer choices D is incorrect because it reflects an element of OSHA 300 but does not encompass the correct title of the log. Answer choice E is incorrect because it refers to one of OSHA's inspection priorities but not to the Log of Work-Related Injuries and Illnesses.

98. B: Organizations typically use the nondisclosure agreement to protect their confidential company information. The lie detector test is only legal within certain boundaries, so answer choice A is incorrect. An employee contract generally binds an employee to the company for a specified length of time, but it does not necessarily protect confidential company information, so answer choice C is incorrect. Organizations utilize video surveillance and random searches to ensure that employees are performing their tasks appropriately, but these activities alone do not protect confidential company information, so answer choices D and E are incorrect.

99. E: Effective substance abuse programs require that drug testing be completely fair, and targeted drug testing for employees who betray substance abuse problems would not necessarily fall under the description of "fair." Answer choices A, B, C, and D are incorrect because all represent components of an effective substance abuse program within an organization.

100. A: As a human resources professional, Angelova's best recommendation would be a counseling program that assists students in recovering from the trauma of a terrorist attack. Answer choice B is incorrect because the human resources professional would not do well to recommend a relocation program for students away from the university. Answer choice C is incorrect because a monthly email newsletter providing recommendations for students would hardly suffice to help students in the aftermath of a terrorist attack. Answer choice D is incorrect because the human resources professional is not generally authorized to advise the creation of a new department. Answer choice E is incorrect because a school-wide emergency response program might be useful in preparing students for a terrorist attack, but it would not necessarily assist them in the aftermath of the attack, and certainly not as well as a counseling program.

Special Report: Additional Bonus Material

Due to our efforts to try to keep this book to a manageable length, we've created a link that will give you access to all of your additional bonus material.

Please visit http://www.mometrix.com/bonus948/phr to access the information.